Are My Blinkers Showing?

Also by Michael York

Accidentally on Purpose

A Shakespearean Actor Prepares (with Adrian Brine)

Dispatches from Armageddon

The first day of filming *Moscow Heat,* with
Alexander (far left) and Sasha (next to me). Hope springs eternal.

Are My Blinkers Showing?

Adventures in Filmmaking in the New Russia

MICHAEL YORK

DA CAPO PRESS
A Member of the Perseus Books Group

Design and composition by Trish Wilkinson
Set in 11.5-point Adobe Garamond

Cataloging-in-Publication data for this book is available from the
Library of Congress.

First Da Capo Press edition 2005
ISBN 0-306-81444-7
ISBN-13 978-0-306-81444-0

Published by Da Capo Press
A Member of the Perseus Books Group
www.dacapopress.com

Da Capo Press books are available at special discounts for bulk purchases
in the U.S. by corporations, institutions, and other organizations. For more
information, please contact the Special Markets Department at the Perseus
Books Group, 11 Cambridge Center, Cambridge, MA 02142, or call (800)
255-1514 or (617) 252-5298, or email special.markets@perseusbooks.com.

1 2 3 4 5 6 7 8 9 — 08 07 06 05

For Pat

Blinkers:
1. Russian garment, as yet unidentified
2. Screening device to ensure monodirectional vision

Russia is a country that no
matter what you say about it, it's true.

— WILL ROGERS

Some people may be Rooshans, and others
may be Prooshans; they are born so, and will please themselves.
Them which is of other naturs thinks different.

— MRS. GAMP IN CHARLES DICKENS'S *MARTIN CHUZZLEWIT*

Contents

Foreword:
A Fly on the Wall

This book evolved out of jottings made both to amuse myself and to assist unreliable memory if I were ever called on to recount the story of filming *Moscow Heat* on location in Russia in 2003, as well as the events preceding its Moscow premiere a year later and its subsequent international release.

After expanding these notes into a longer form, I was surprised at how much the resulting narrative presented a study in contrasts. It was about the city observed as the capital of communism thirty years ago, and as it is now in its renewed capitalist incarnation, with my experience of the Soviet era set against that of contemporary times. It was about Russia as much as about Moscow.

Not least these pages highlight two ways of working that came into contact, and occasional conflict, in the lively arena of a movie set. Sparks were struck, sometimes producing merely noxious, obscuring smoke, but often an attractive, illuminating flame. American ways of filmmaking are contrasted with those of my Russian hosts, charting both where these differences converged to provide delightful fellowship and mutual understanding and where they diverged, causing misunderstandings and recriminations.

It's also a comparison between myself as a young actor, out to conquer the world, making a beachhead at the Moscow Film Festival in 1973, and my later, perhaps wiser, self where every new role was placed in the larger context of accumulated experience.

My viewpoint was that of a privileged fly on the wall, for the most part feasting contentedly on the riches found in abundance and at other times buzzing indignantly when swatted by fate. Flies, at least, are renowned for their extraordinary vision, and I have tried to see as much as I could. With glimpses back to the turbulent past and forward to the uncertain future, I have set these observations in as wide a perspective as possible. *Moscow Heat* captures not only a fast-paced story but also a moment in time, although I realize that, as much as I have tried to bottle up this zeitgeist, much remains elusive or hidden in plain sight.

The book concerns both this particular film and my experience of movies in general, but I would like to think it might appeal as much to the student of human nature as to the cinephile.

Each film project encapsulates a brief lifetime, different from any that precedes it or any that will follow. It has a print of uniqueness as if, each time one goes before the camera, inherent genes are rearranged to produce something at the same time familiar, yet strikingly different.

This was certainly the case with *Moscow Heat,* an essentially Russian film made in English with a mixed cast and crew of natives and Americans, with a few other nationalities thrown in to enliven the already volatile mixture. Whenever I see it, the movie unleashes vivid memories of a damp summer when the world heaved a collective sigh of relief that it had so far survived the new threat of rogue nuclear terrorism—a key plot element of our film—and held its breath that this situation would persist and, if international understanding continued to evolve, actually improve.

Russia is still the mysterious enigma of Winston Churchill's famous description, all the more puzzling as, on the surface, we all seem so similar. The arts, however, are one of the few things that we do have in common, where we speak the same language, albeit with charmingly different accents.

Today events in Russia are too important to be ignored. Once the czar coughed and only Russia caught a cold. Today the whole world is prey to infection. I hope at least that these accumulated observations will give some measure of illumination and, at the same time—what our film essentially aims to provide—entertainment.

Los Angeles
May 2005

PART ONE

Camera!

My humble trailer in front of one of
Stalin's grandiose ziggurats.

Один · 1

Nobody Knows Anything

Paper is patient — you can put anything on it.
— RUSSIAN PROVERB

I heard it through the grapevine. Word of a feature film to be made in Russia, in English, began to filter through in the early summer of 2003. Called *Moscow Heat,* it was but one item on a list of movies slated for imminent production. "A retired diplomat and a police detective, seeking justice, pursue a gunrunner to Moscow," a précis of the plot promisingly announced. "When the detective is wounded and the diplomat is arrested and assigned to a Russian policeman for deportation, he becomes an unlikely accomplice as they exact their revenge upon a black market arms dealer. Shooting from late July/early August in Moscow."

Although warming immediately to this fish-out-of-water scenario, I harbored concerns about the grapevine's reliability. In the early 1970s, for example, talk of a film version of the stage musical *Cabaret* was similarly bruited about London. I investigated, only to find that they were looking for a "Michael York type" for the Herr Issyvoo role! Asking my agent if he thought I could possibly pass as such an individual, my persistence was rewarded, as that film provided one of my happiest professional experiences.

In the case of the Russian movie, no such preconceived identity was requested, although the diplomat was specified as a Briton based in the United States. This made it even more appealing because it reflected my own experience of being raised in England but, for the past thirty years, living in Hollywood—or Gollywood, as the Russians style it, the delightful result of the foreign *h* sound being rendered as *g*.

A request to read the screenplay resulted in its eventual arrival bearing the handsome, historically charged double eagle logo of Czar Pictures. The fact that the production company was based in Moscow made the project even more alluring. The script brought with it a welcome whiff of foreign romance and travel, of adventure and discovery, with a heady overtone of vintage John le Carré. Opening any script for the first time is fraught with consequence. It could change one's life—or it could merely be another unremarkable stop along one's unpredictable career path.

A cursory perusal revealed a scenario that was strong on character as well as action. After a brief prelude in America, the bulk of the story took place in Moscow. A press release attached to the script elaborated further: "A criminal gang of weapons dealers in the US kills a policeman. His partner Rudy asks the father of the murdered cop—Roger Chambers, a retired British secret service agent—to help him find the killers, who are hiding in Russia. Disguised as tourists, the two of them take off for Russia."

I must confess to being easily seduced by locations. Any movie that is set in foreign parts will send my pulse racing. As a result, I have filmed all over the world, relishing this peripatetic aspect of the work—even when stranded for months in some improbable, inhospitable place. I regard it as a privilege to know such countries as India, Australia, Brazil, and, yes, even the United States from being "on location."

In this I am fortunate to be married to a wife, Pat, who shares the same enthusiasm for fresh fields and pastures new. She was the travel editor of *Glamour* magazine in that civilized interim before deregulation and international terror turned travel into a mass-marketed, sardine-canned endurance feat. I like to think my job has given her present work as a freelance fine art photographer an extra dimension and scope. Ever since we married in 1968, we have embraced this gadabout life. Our digs have included castles in Ireland, mansions in Texas, *ryokans* in Japan, boats in the Caribbean, and enough hotel rooms to make a Michelin Guide inspector giddy.

Not every actor feels this way. I recall our incredulity at a leading lady with whom I was once filming in India, who declined an invitation to accompany us to see the local sights. Her husband was being sent out with a movie camera, she explained, so that she could view them in comfort back home in England.

Russia has always exerted a strong appeal, and not just because I grew up in its ominous shadow during the Cold War. Fascinated as a schoolboy by our monolithic enemy, I briefly subscribed to a newspaper—no doubt freely distributed—that trumpeted the glorious Soviet achievements that were crowned by the world-encircling triumph of *Sputnik*. We heard the signal on our little transistor radios and feared the realization of something hitherto confined to our comic books—a conquest from space. Such paranoia was fed by reading the latest James Bond novel, *From Russia with Love*, where Ian Fleming's debonair Englishman saves the world from unspeakable horrors dealt by his nemesis, SMERSH, the dreaded Soviet organ of vengeance.

A study of Russian literature engendered further curiosity about this passionate, complex people; my discovery of their theater and cinema only strengthened this attraction. The British have always revered Anton Chekhov as an unofficial countryman, just as Russians claim William Shakespeare as theirs. Charlie Chaplin, pioneering the same new medium, declared Sergei Eisenstein's *Battleship Potemkin* to be the best film in the world, and it happened to be one of the first silent movies I ever saw.

Later I caught up with Eisenstein's heroic epic about the warrior prince Alexander Nevsky, who coincidentally shared the same name as one of *Moscow Heat's* Russian producers and lead actors. My window on the East was opened wider with such masterpieces as Aleksandr Dovzhenko's *Earth,* Mikhail Kalatozov's *The Cranes Are Flying,* and Grigori Kozintzev's great film versions of *Hamlet* and *King Lear.* These last two were translated by Boris Pasternak; his *Dr. Zhivago,* both the epic novel and the Hollywood epic, also made an indelible impression.

So when I was first asked to visit Russia in 1971, the invitation, with its strange Cyrillic script and stamp, had a talismanic significance. There was no question of not accepting, even though my visit was inconvenient and rushed. I simply had to go. In the same way, I had traveled to apartheid-riven South Africa when it was unfashionable, nay unacceptable, to do so. I wanted to see it for myself rather than recycle conventional, secondhand truths. Now I had a similar powerful sense that in doing so, I was crossing a line to feast with enemies. Curiously, on arrival in Moscow, I experienced another overwhelming sensation—that of having been there before. Perhaps it is not without significance that I am frequently mistaken for being Russian. The English writer Alan Bennett once sent me a postcard of some Russian steelworkers in Pittsburgh at the turn of the century—and there I am staring out of it.

I have also filmed extensively in countries that were formerly part of the Communist bloc, such as Hungary and Czechoslovakia.

The old Yugoslavia was a popular and inexpensive film location boasting a variety of scenery, although many considered working there the cinematic equivalent of being sent to the gulag. There was a mischievous myth among British actors during the 1970s that if cast in such a film, you could contact a Yugoslavs Anonymous hotline and be talked out of it!

There was also another story—this time true—about a film made in Russia with a large number of limey actors. Garrisoned in rather primitive circumstances on the remote steppe, they had their morale saved by one of the company who had been a prisoner of war in World War II. He organized them as if they were in a prison camp, with each inmate assigned specific duties, thereby establishing an esprit de corps that got everyone through until eventual liberation.

Although my family lacked immediate connections with Russia, apart from a Derbyshire ancestor, James Higginbottom, who gained fame in St. Petersburg as an engraver, I had the good fortune to meet several of its more interesting citizens. In particular, while filming *The Taming of the Shrew* in Rome in 1966, I was introduced to Rudolf Nureyev, then the wild boy darling of the ballet world, having made his famous "leap to the West" from Leningrad's Kirov Company five years before. There was a superficial resemblance between us, and the following year, I was asked to return to Rome to audition for the role of a certain defecting Russian ballet dancer. This blatant exploitation of the Nureyev legend came to nothing—yet another among the ghostly legion of unmade film projects—and I was rather relieved. Decades later, Roger Vadim, himself of Russian extraction, asked me to play another equally charismatic artist. This time it was Ilya, a passionate musician who took as much pleasure in conducting love affairs as orchestras.

Instinct, as much as anything, plays a major role in the choice of roles. After all, there is no blueprint for an acting career, no set path through the jungle. The famous adage that in Hollywood, "nobody knows anything" has a disconcerting yet comforting ring of truth, so that the outcome of any venture (even stellar and expensive ones) is as much in doubt as the fate awaiting the most modest independent film. So, requesting my agent to pursue an offer for *Moscow Heat,* I left in mid-July for a few days in the redwood forests north of San Francisco, having been invited to stay in a cabin there with friends.

I spent the flight to Oakland reviewing the film script again, my initial positive reaction being confirmed. It had the potential to be more than the sum of its parts, and ideas for it, I found, were flowing freely. "Is that the new Austin Powers film?" the young girl sitting next to me inquired through a thicket of braces. It reminded me how the first script in this shagadelic saga had given little hint of its stupendous potential. But there had been something about it that made me sign on to play that other diplomatic Brit, Basil Exposition, and in this case instinct served me well.

Calling my agent from the airport, I learned of his reaction. Similarly impressed, he gave me the telephone number of the film's director, Jeff Celentano, whom I agreed to call for further discussion. Then I drove over the Bay, through neat suburbs and up through vineyards and forests to enter the green fastness of redwood groves. Our encampment was by the Russian River, another good omen. Once there, cell phones became signal-less, so all further deal making was done through the occasional pay phone call. Being unable to leave a callback number, I rather hoped this involuntary hard-to-get tactic might raise any financial offer then being negotiated.

On my return to LA, I met with Jeff Celentano, who turned out to be a surfer as well as cineaste with a suitably laid-back demeanor. Some of his locations remained to be found, he revealed, but there was talk of being allowed to film in the Kremlin. John Aronson, a frequent collaborator, would again be his cinematographer, and Jeff gave me a copy of a recent film, *Gunshy,* to more fully appreciate their work.

Reluctantly curtailing our conversation, I left for an appointment in Hollywood, where a producer friend, Mace Neufeld, was receiving a star on the Walk of Fame. Mace, incidentally, was a veteran of the Russian campaign, having filmed *The Saint* there with Val Kilmer as recently as 1997. I hoped for a chance to get some practical advice. Perhaps propitiously, my phone rang in the middle of the ceremony, confirming that the proposed deal for my services was now agreed.

That evening Pat and I watched *Gunshy* and were impressed. The action sequences were exciting yet didn't overwhelm the acting. Jeff was a former actor and probably knew from personal experience how to optimize performances. The film's production values were far in excess of its modest $2 million budget, and John Aronson's cinematography, in particular, was outstanding. All this boded well for *Moscow Heat,* the biggest independent film in Russian movie history, with a budget reputed to be around $10 million.

The following day a contract was finalized, replete with all the arcana peculiar to such documents—notably, size of billing, trailer, accommodation, and airline seat. "While on location in Russia," the fine print stipulated, "Mr. York will attend a Press Conference, do at least 3 Television Shows and 3 interviews (magazines, newspapers, etc.)." Even though we would be filming in midsummer, and its relevance to the story was questionable, the comforting pledge was also made that there would be "no nudity or doubling for nudity."

The only drawback was that the production company was asking for a two-week leeway for the start of filming. Pat had an important show opening at the Academy of Motion Picture Arts and

Sciences in Los Angeles on September 12, and I wanted to be there to support her. If we kept to the proposed start date of August 11, I could just make it back in time for the festivities.

As already mentioned, my cop co-star and also executive producer of the film was the autocratically named Alexander Nevsky. A famous bodybuilder and a former Mr. World, he had even written a book called *How to Become a Schwarzenegger in Russia*. Trading bulk for the boards, he had now followed his idol into the acting business. Looking him up on his website, I found not only several photographs, including one of him brandishing muscles and a gun outside the Moscow White House, but also some interesting personal details. For the past ten years he had pioneered a campaign to outlaw the use of steroids in sport. In addition, he had "four published books, a weekly radio show, a top-rated TV program and a PhD in Economics." Now dividing his time between Moscow and Los Angeles, Alexander had already appeared in small roles in several American movies. On the other side of the critical fence, he was also a member of the influential Hollywood Foreign Press Association, the presenters of the Golden Globe Awards.

There was also a photo of his Moscow-based co-producer, Alexander Izotov, meeting with the speaker of the Duma, the Russian parliament. So these were not provincial nobodies cobbling together a project to launch their careers. They had already collaborated on a movie about bodybuilding, and Jeff confirmed that Alexander indeed had a compelling quality on screen. He was still hoping to start filming soon, which galvanized me into applying for the necessary visas from the Russian consulate in San Francisco, the only one west of the Mississippi.

Two days later, Jeff called with an upbeat progress report. Adrian Paul, who had starred in the *Highlander* TV series, was cast to play my doomed son. Moreover, the respected director Tony Leung, who was also chairman of the Hong Kong Stuntman's Association, had agreed to choreograph the action sequences—to give them extra style, impact, and presence. I mentally added more laps to my daily workout in the pool. The big problem, Jeff reported, was that dealing with Moscow was a logistical nightmare. Because LA lagged eleven long hours behind, it meant staying up until the small hours of the morning in order to communicate with the Russian production office just as they started their day. We agreed to meet for lunch to discuss things further.

Over the inevitable pasta and Pellegrino, we talked about character and costume, motivation and method, and found ourselves in general agreement. We debated whether Roger Chambers, as a diplomat and an Englishman, would want to be armed, as per the script, and I resolved to try and work in a certain reluctance, reflecting as it did my own proclivities. The accessibility and profusion of guns in the United States, all justified by an antique clause in a colonial document written with a feather, is one of the things that truly scares me about living there. And yet American politicians wax indignant about the same weapons proliferating in other countries. Our own messy act, I suggest, requires cleaning up first.

Among other suggestions was that perhaps father and son could be quarreling at the outset. This is an old Shakespearean trick that the Bard used to grab an audience's attention at the beginning and heighten energy. In our film it would also serve to make the son's death more poignant and his father's strong response more plausible. I thought there were too many male characters and too much testosterone—at least one of the Russian police officers, for example, could be played by a woman. Ray Bradbury, nattily dressed in shirt and tie on top of minuscule white shorts, was lunching nearby. "Tell them to send me the royalties they owe me!" he urged on discovering that we were Moscow bound.

The following day I contacted Robert Madrid, who was wearing three hats in this venture—writer, co-producer, and actor. Cast as Rudy, my son's cop buddy, he sounded amiable and enthusiastic. When I discussed ideas for the script, he seemed receptive to many of them. He mentioned, however, that the Russians had already said *nyet* to my suggestion of a female cop because I would have to spike her drink with shampoo at a crucial point when escaping from police detention. This was deemed far too ungallant for my character!

Robert also reported that the Russians, in retaliation for the difficulties they were experiencing from the Americans in the post-9/11 climate, were apparently going slow on U.S. visa applications. And we were supposed to be leaving in a few days. Like Chekhov's three sisters, I began to wonder if we would ever get to Moscow. But there was a thread of hope: Russian consulates abroad apparently had to live on their income from issuing visas, so sheer economics dictated that we would eventually obtain them sometime, somewhere.

For the next few days while recording a BBC radio play, I made innumerable phone calls to check the status of our documents. Despite this era of electronic immediacy, I eventually learned that approval had been dispatched by telex. It seemed incredible that such Cold War–era communication still existed. We were advised to cut our losses and reapply for our papers the following week in Stockholm, where I had long been scheduled to perform the Tennyson/Strauss "Enoch Arden" in a recital en route to Moscow.

With the application of a little further exasperated pressure, it was conceded that they could be sent by mail. Eventually Robert kindly arranged for a courier to pick up the documents, which, like an old Soviet agent doing a spy drop, he then hand-delivered. This triumphant scene took place at a Beverly Hills dinner party, Robert having received the permits a scant hour before.

The next morning Pat and I rose before dawn to do all those things that had to be done before our afternoon departure. I habitually leave packing until the last moment to prevent dithering over choices. Seeing Pat's carelessly crammed bags, I'm always amused to think that she once penned earnest columns in *Glamour* magazine about how a young lady correctly packed a suitcase. But now she was still preoccupied in selecting images to be digitally printed for her Academy exhibition. The continuing demands the show made meant that, sadly, she would not be able to stay long with me in Russia. We were still making arrangements by phone in the departure lounge before our 747 finally lumbered off to Europe, taking me back to Russia on the thirty-second anniversary of my first visit there.

En route, London greeted us with several days of unusually warm sunshine. We then flew on to Sweden for the performances, first at an arts festival amid the rocky fjords of the west coast, and then in sea-girt Stockholm. Here we received news that the film had been delayed a week. Where to go? What to do? A return to London was a possibility, except that England was now sweltering under the same intolerable 90-degree heat wave that seemed to be baking most of Europe. Staying put was an enticing option, as there was still so much of this Venice of the North to explore.

Eventually we decided to press on. The delay would provide an invaluable opportunity to get settled and start preparations. Besides, Pat was anxious to see a little more of Russia before returning to complete her exhibition. At Stockholm's Arlanda airport there was perhaps a foretaste of things to come. Getting her return flight from Moscow delayed to maximize our time together, we confronted a stern lady Aeroflot agent who scrutinized Pat suspiciously as if she had just asked to bring a bomb on board. A notice prominent on the desk explained: "If we are not smiling, we are just working hard to make you smile!"

I once heard a rumor that Aeroflot had to instigate a "smile at the customer" campaign. Why is it that Russians are disinclined to smile? Is it the residue of some bygone order of Peter the Great, like his banning of beards, or the result of so many violent political swings? Or is it simply a component of their famous stoic fatalism? The reason lay waiting to be discovered.

Buying disposable cameras and other supplies, I little realized how ridiculously redundant this was, and what bounty awaited us at our destination. My most significant purchase, however, was a little notebook. I had a half-formed idea to keep an informal journal about the experience that lay ahead, anticipating that it would be memorable, challenging, and hopefully noteworthy.

Два · 2

Red Is Still Beautiful

Moscow: how much there is in that sound.
— ALEXANDER PUSHKIN

Threading through towering thunderstorms, our plane heads over the Baltic in the direction that Napoleon, Hitler, and so many other ambitious invaders had taken before. A welcoming sun floods the scene as we disembark at Sheremetyevo, one of the five airports around Moscow, Europe's biggest city, in Russia, the largest country in the world.

Joining the long line at passport control, I think of the young doctor we met in Los Angeles who left Russia as a teenager. The hardest habit to lose, she confided, was using her elbows to get ahead of others, a practice ingrained by her parents. An attractive, uniformed girl—a change from the suspicious military personnel of the past—welcomes us. Bags are retrieved and we move through customs, greeted by a long-haired young man who introduces himself as Vlad. Bouquets are presented, and we are ushered to a waiting group of journalists and photographers who explode into flashing action. I make some platitudinous statement to the TV camera about the importance of co-productions in international understanding and say how much I'm looking forward to getting to know the new Russia. Is this the first of my contractual interviews, I idly wonder? More flashbulbs mark our progress outside, where a white limousine awaits. Once encushioned and on our way, we try to converse with Vlad, who sits way up front with the driver, but the distance between us and the almost continual ringing of his cell phone defeat any meaningful exchange. Anyway, we are happy to sit and peer through the darkened glass at the brave new world outside.

There are definite changes to be seen. Construction is everywhere, and advertisements shout and blandish from all quarters. There is a plethora of new malls—including a purple one—as well as that other visitor newly arrived from Sweden with much ultramodern baggage, eastern Europe's biggest shopping and entertainment center, the giant Ikea emporium. It all looks brighter and more confident. The well-dressed crowds—there's hardly a headscarf in sight—are enjoying their early August weekend.

As a banner on its facade proclaims, the National Hotel is celebrating its hundredth birthday. Now taken over by the Meridien chain—a sign of the internationalism currently sweeping Russia—its young, efficient employees, speaking impeccable English, bustle and, yes, smile. What a world away from Soviet times when grim, ancient crones inhabited every hotel floor, scrutinizing each coming and going. As a notice in a hotel of that era proclaimed: "If this is your first visit to the USSR, you are welcome to it."

We check into a suite on the National's fourth floor, with spectacular views of the Kremlin's domes and crenellations. The furnishings are traditional with walls of pale lilac, the Czarina Alexandra's favorite color and the same hue as the exquisite Fabergé cufflinks that Pat gave me as a wedding present. It all looks very familiar. We are almost certain that these were our rooms when we last stayed here in July 1999. The living room has a large dining table that could double for work. There is a little vestibule behind etched glass doors with a substantial coatrack built to accommodate large fur coats, capes, and hats. The hotel's past is still present in the old-fashioned monogram woven into the carpet and emblazoned even on bathrobes.

Depositing our bags, we go outside to maintain what has become a ritual for us on arriving in Moscow: a renewed visit to Krasnaya Ploshchad, Red Square. Only a few paces from the hotel, the huge historic space is still exactly as depicted on the lacquer box I purchased on that first visit to Moscow. The only difference is that now the Romanoff double eagle has replaced the steeple-topping red stars, and there's been some rebuilding of structures that the Communists tore down to facilitate the entry of military parades, replete with huge ballistic missiles. In particular, the beautifully restored Resurrection Gate now frames a grand entry to a square that today seems unusually empty. We discover that it has been cordoned off and partly closed—because of Chechen terrorism, a passerby informs us. Lenin, that archterrorist, looks even more isolated in his lonely tomb.

Only a few months before, Paul McCartney had played here, with President Vladimir Putin among his enthusiastic audience. The event represented a historic rapprochement, as the Soviets had banned the decadent Beatles from performing in their sacred square. Putin, in best ex-KGB mode, explained that the Fab Four's music was considered "propaganda of an alien ideology." Sir Paul himself confided that, even though he co-wrote such hits as "Back in the USSR," he did not know much about the country. Like me, he regarded it as "a mystical land."

Our disappointment is tempered by the fact that at least St. Basil's Cathedral, that quintessence of Russian flamboyance and mystery, is still accessible. Commemorating the defeat of the Tartars rather than more godly triumphs, it is newly restored in all its poly-chrome splendor. Each exuberant onion dome resembles a pendant Christmas bauble. No wonder Ivan the Terrible blinded the architect of this oriental fantasy, not wanting any replication to mar its uniqueness. An equally colorful rainbow now hangs over the deserted square. Is it a symbol for the film? Stormy weather ahead, or maybe a crock of gold at the end of it?

A top-hatted, frock-coated doorman welcomes us back inside the hotel, where we indulge in a supper of blinis and caviar. The latter seems less abundant in these polluted and overfished times: will it end up a fond gastronomical memory, a dodo delicacy? For Pat, caviar evokes memories as powerful as those conjured up by Marcel Proust's modest madeleine. Here in the mid-1960s on assignment for *Glamour* in the dead of winter, she consumed it at every meal. It kept her completely free of the colds, she claims, which plagued her colleagues. At one of these repasts she encountered Dominique Lapierre, then on assignment for *Paris Match* magazine. A journalist for whom the word *nyet* was meaningless and to whom no door remained long closed, he invited Pat to see his Moscow. They went everywhere and met everyone, from the ballerina Maya Plisetskaya to a surgeon who was attaching a second head to a dog!

The next morning, we are greeted by a huge breakfast buffet that is served by chefs wearing toques and caters to every imaginable taste. The gracious staff favors us with a table by the vast picture windows affording panoramic views of the jammed traffic fighting its way to work below, as well as the Moskva Hotel opposite. After serving apparatchiks and tourists for the past seventy years and immortalizing itself on the Stolichnaya vodka label, the Moskva has just closed. Like a Christo work of art, its bulk is almost entirely wrapped in gargantuan posters for BMW cars and a radio station.

The strange design of the building resulted when Stalin commissioned two different architectural plans and unfortunately
signed off on both. Because no one dared risk his lethal displeasure, the two were uncomfortably blended into one. The year
2003, as it happens, marks the fiftieth anniversary of the tyrant's
death. If only walls could talk! And these gray, dour ones were certainly bugged. Pat recalls that on her earlier 1960s trip, she complained to a companion about the lack of towels in her suite. Just
moments later, a knock on the door revealed a maid burdened
with an armful of fresh ones.

Having tried to call home last night and run afoul of the room
phone's inability to coax a reluctant California answering machine
into living up to its name, I decide that, like Vlad and two-thirds
of the Muscovites already observed, I must have a cell phone.
Luckily I have with me an uncomplicated one bought in Italy last
year for the same reason. Now I assume it is merely a question of
changing its chip and signing up with a local phone company.

This transaction, however, at the nearby Megafon store, with its
glass floor inlaid with every kind of communications equipment
like a frozen phone lake, demands over an hour of our time as rates
and plans are laboriously explained. A passport, as well as patience,
is required to sign up, reminding me of the elaborate customs formalities, the *deklaratsia*, we had undergone the previous day, with
forms in duplicate and everything having to be scrupulously declared. The long shadow of bureaucracy seems to hover over the
bright new business world.

Another echo of past times resounds when Pat is inexplicably refused permission to photograph a particularly beautiful girl who is
sitting unself-consciously in the sunshine by the store's window. At
the same time, my cell phone is derided as too simple and old-
fashioned. Russians prefer all the latest bells and whistles. Here the
cell phone is not so much a means of communication as a status

symbol—as a car is in the West. In an updating of seventeenth-century tulip mania, people risk bankruptcy to obtain the latest luxurious models to add to the several they already own. Apparently there's a new Escada-styled phone that costs a mere $1,000.

Moscow, as well as Rome, is reputed to be built on seven hills, although they are not much in evidence from where we stand. Like so many other ancient capitals, a river runs through it, which the Viking hordes sailed down to found their stockaded outpost. Establishing itself at the crossroads of commerce, the city's subsequent settlement led eventually to a series of ring roads encircling the center—even the subway map looks like a round target. We are now at the bull's-eye.

It's an enticingly beautiful day, so we decide to go for a long walk. Heading west, we make our first stop at the Manezh building by the Kremlin. A onetime imperial cavalry stable that resembles a classic Greek temple, it has now been converted to an exhibition space. Pat's photographic show was successfully held here four years ago. Slowly deciphering the Cyrillic letters spelling out our route, we continue on after lingering outside in the welcome shade of the huge Cathedral of Christ the Savior. This shiny, brand-new building is an exact replica of the one torn down by Stalin and replaced by a giant font—the world's largest swimming pool.

Everywhere there is a sense that an era of secularism is being rapidly replaced by one of renewed religious fervor, although I hear that Moscow is still home to over thirty satanic cults. We join an old-fashioned queue to get through the sadly now omnipresent metal detector into the vast building. With its towering, glittering iconostasis—a wall of tiered saints—there seems to be enough ambient gold and silver to set off myriad alarms. Head-scarved little old ladies ecstatically kiss these holy portraits, and we marvel how they managed to keep the flame alive during the long atheist winter.

Farther west lies the House of Photography, situated on several converted floors of a modest house. The artist principally featured is the legendary Lev Borodulin, whose eightieth birthday is being celebrated with a major retrospective. The glory days of Soviet sport are depicted in triumphalist photos of phalanxes of flag-waving athletes, stepping out to conquer the world with their discipline and square-jawed fervor. Impressive as these are, I prefer his simpler, more human shots of people laughing in the street, of children playing: life just happening, rather than on self-conscious parade.

That evening we dine on the chic, modern rooftop of the Hyatt Hotel, overlooking the pink crepuscular city and the even pinker Bolshoi theater on Teatralnaya Square. Refusing to let me pay, the restaurant manager cites the pleasure that some of my work has given him. Such moments are to be treasured. I remember my first visit to Moscow coincided with the Russian release of the famed BBC television production of *The Forsyte Saga* in back-to-back formula, with my three episodes as Young Jolly being shown during the week of my visit. Even more gratifying than the fact that this saga of bourgeois British capitalism should be so eagerly consumed by the progeny of Marx and Lenin were the little bouquets spontaneously presented to me in the street. Artists were respected, as they still are, and we lucky visitors were then the beneficiaries of this bounty.

In Old Russian, the word "red" also meant "beautiful," and Red Square fully lives up to this latter interpretation when we return for an evening stroll, enjoying on the way a string quartet and a singer performing sonorously in the underpass. Outside restaurants, costumed Boyars and Cossacks coax passersby inside. Everything is remarkably clean, with trucks regularly hosing down the streets. Marshall Zhukov, mounted in effigy on a horse rather than a tank, having swept away the Nazi invaders, now supervises the army of uniformed cleaners who have replaced the old broom-wielding babushkas. The weekend is a big time for marriages, the square a lucky place, and white-gowned brides haunt the scene like refugees from a Chagall painting.

There is one sad, sobering sight, though. The collapse of the Soviet Union's social security system, under which pensioners were reasonably well off, has meant that many have had to swallow their dignity and come here to sell goods to enable them to survive on their now almost worthless pensions of around $50 a month, and even less in the provinces. Old ladies hawk cans of beer and cigarettes, finding ready takers. Apparently the endemic alcohol problem has only worsened with the burgeoning prosperity that replaced the old fatalism. Russians are drinking more and dying at an even earlier age—on average at fifty-nine instead of sixty-one. Fifty percent of all Russian men now expire before retirement, whereas the figure in the United States is a mere 15 percent.

I was reminded of visiting Yalta in 1994 not long after the Soviet system collapsed and being infinitely moved by the sight of classically trained musicians busking with their children in the streets for kopeks. Now a small crowd throws these same kopeks away, tossing them backward over their heads into a brass circle embedded in the cobbles—apparently to guarantee their return.

The newspaper next morning reports that London is sweltering under record 101-degree heat. In fact, Moscow seems to be the one cool place in Europe. It has had a soggy summer so far, with slumping ice cream sales. So much for Moscow heat! Having a lunch date with Jeff Celentano at our hotel, we spend the morning just over the road in the State History Museum, a red-brick bastion of portentousness. Inside there's everything from the Stone Age to the space age on display, with each gallery decorated accordingly. A wartime Yak aircraft makes a particular impression: it saved the world for democracy as well as communism.

Jeff is with Anastasia, one of the bright, young English-speaking assistants who, like Vlad, have been coopted into this production. Their translation skills, not to mention their enthusiasm, are proving invaluable. Over lunch Jeff reports on the various issues that have slowed preproduction, mostly caused by the need to mesh Russian and American work habits and filming techniques. There are frequent misunderstandings, not a few of them caused by the fact that the Russian and the American scripts differ in significant detail.

A certain dogged literalness also prevails. Finding himself, for example, being slowly driven along the jammed road to the airport on a location search, Jeff asked why. "Script says, 'Road to the Airport,'" came the reply, prompting his exasperated response that any road would do and preferably one without potholes or traffic lights where other vehicular action could be filmed. The concept of doubling locations is also not much employed.

Jeff mentions that the car chase—mandatory, it seems, to almost all action films—has been changed to a much more interesting one in boats on the Moscow River. This is an excellent idea because it will enable us to feature all the recent riverside embellishments. Had he not been locked in to some performers' contractual dates, Jeff tells me, he would have delayed the film's start further. I breathe a secret sigh of relief.

Later that afternoon Pat and I explore the National's labyrinthine facilities. Pat wants to find the rooms where she stayed on her first visit. Meals then could only be purchased with prepaid coupons, but as the recipient of so much generous hospitality, she was unable to spend a single one. So she blew them all on a great farewell party in her suite. A piano was moved in, and revolutionary songs were sung far into the night, as vodka, caviar, beef Wellington, and, of all things, Baked Alaska were served. The piano, we discover, is still there, although now probably reduced to accompanying sentimental love ballads rather than world-shaping anthems. We also find a wonderfully situated rooftop pool, providing the unusual possibility of swimming within sight of Red Square.

Afterward I have a costume fitting. Like a replay of the famous Marx Brothers cabin scene from *Night at the Opera,* many people cram into our living room, including Jeff, the wardrobe mistress, and even more assistants to the assistants. Annie, cinematographer John Aronson's wife, is also there. A professional costume designer, she has been coopted by Jeff. Fortunately Natasha, her elegant Russian counterpart, has prepared well, and the first suit I try on fits, as does a suede jacket that looks absurdly hot in the present climate. It does, however, seem more appropriate for a diplomat than the hip, Prada-type clothes that Jeff is advocating.

The shoes provided are smart—fortunately not the pointy-toed horrors in current vogue that remind me of Rosa Klebb's assassination shoes in *From Russia with Love.* But their soles are leather, and anticipating all the running around that lies ahead, I make a mental note to buy my own rubber-soled ones. Comfortable footwear is fundamental for any performance, and the stores seem to be overflowing with choices, a far cry from the time when vinyl shoes shod the nation. Moreover, I can wear my own watch and keep my wedding ring—no more soapy, increasingly stubborn, attempts to squeeze it off. There are no stifling wigs to wear or even tooth fillings to white out, as was required for my John the Baptist's crying in the wilderness in *Jesus of Nazareth.* An actor performs better when certain that his costume is correct, thereby avoiding a subconscious neurosis similar to that experienced by the man who, getting up to speak in public, is convinced that his fly is undone.

I'm asked to film a TV show outside in the streets tomorrow and bow to my contractual obligations. A printed schedule for the entire shoot is delivered, and to our disappointment, I learn that I will now definitely be unable to return home in time for Pat's opening. Back there in LA, the temperature is reported to be over 100 degrees, while here next morning it's raining hard, which swiftly squelches that outdoor TV interview.

We decide to spend the day indoors at the Tretyakov Gallery. Its collection of icons is particularly celebrated, their return now insistently demanded by the resurgent Orthodox Church. I feel a fleeting pang of guilt about the icon we bought from a taxi driver who stopped for us on our 1973 trip in a similar driving rain, "only because I like your face." Apparently he was paid whether or not he picked up passengers. Furtively parking in a dark street, he pulled it out from under his seat. Taking a gamble, I traded it for my watch and all the cash we were carrying, little realizing that I could have been arrested for this transaction. The exquisitely enameled icon turned out to be as authentic as it was beautiful and has given serene pleasure in the intervening years.

The Tretyakov boasts acres of art from the eleventh to the twentieth centuries. All sixty canvas-crammed rooms are equally jammed with visitors. Many seem to be cruise ship passengers, stranded strangely far inland, obediently following their guides who compete in a Babel of languages for their attention. Pat and I are mesmerized by the giant paintings of the great nineteenth-century artist Ilya Repin, which have a cinematic immediacy and drama. I'm also particularly drawn to the portrait by Osip Braz of another personal hero, Anton Chekhov. Seeing him at eye level seems more appropriate than craning up at his statue outside the Moscow Art Theater. Chekhov would probably have hated it, being a humanist, not a monumentalist. Before completing the full tour, we are both visually exhausted and vow to return and do it all in reverse.

The rain abates in the afternoon, allowing us to venture out. Drainpipes here are enormous, dealing easily with these inundations and giving promise of roofs heavy with the snows of the

coming season. In the *perekhod*, or underpass, amid the shops and
bars, we find my kind of treasure—a little kiosk selling nothing
but teas. Other street vendors outside sell fruit piled in mouth-
watering profusion like the still lives depicted in the Old Master
paintings we have just enjoyed. Walking past the pastel-shaded
walls of Moscow University, we arrive at the little rotunda fountain with its charming statues of the writer Alexander Pushkin and
his beloved Natalia Goncharova.

Just as Muscovites have been doing since the eighteenth century, we promenade along the tree-lined Tverskoy bulvar, passing
elegant classic mansions, including the East-West Hotel, where
several of our crew are staying, and the ones now housing the
Pushkin Drama Theater, with students learning lines outside.
The vibrant colors of the renovated buildings are unexpected. I've
seen several movies about Moscow that have been shot in Madrid,
Prague, Toronto, Montreal—even Dundee—and they mostly get
it wrong by playing up the gloomy granite rather than these airy
stucco fantasies.

The looming modern pile of the New Moscow Art Theater,
however, one of the city's seventy-two theaters, is a rude intrusion
into the prevailing classical sobriety. I was glad to learn that after
an uneasy period of adjustment, unsubsidized theater is now
booming, maintaining one of the great glories of Russian culture.
Cuts in government funding, moreover, have meant less official
interference in the arts. As in the West, this situation has led to a
lively debate about how far private funding and market pressures
should be allowed to erode the old classical repertory system.

Stopped on the street, we are invited by the proud owner to inspect his sumptuous new Italian restaurant, full of gilded gon-
dolas, grottoes, and damask drapes, with bathrooms like small
Renaissance chapels. Inside businessmen huddle over deals like

consiglieri plotting vendettas. As the guidebook informs us, apparently unsuperstitious about the nature of such a devilish number, this is but one of Moscow's 6,660 hostelries.

We finish up outside another, the Café Pushkin, where on our last visit, we had the pleasure of dining on its superb Russian cuisine with the distinguished director Nikita Mikhalkov and Vanessa Redgrave, both in town for the film festival. Situated on four floors of a nineteenth-century house, with waiters dressed in costumes of that era, the restaurant has a menu written in Old Russian—but with distinctly modern prices. It also boasts a collection of seven thousand antique books. Are they cookbooks or all penned by Pushkin, I idly wonder, and can they be browsed along with the borscht?

Crossing the Pushkinskaya *ploshchad,* we turn and head toward the Kremlin, down the slope of Tverskaya *ulitsa,* the main road to the north. Passing the mayor's imposing office as well as some busy stores and restaurants, we return to the National Hotel, which has anchored the bottom right-hand corner of the street for the past turbulent century.

That evening we meet for dinner with the two Alexanders, our producers, who in the delightful, time-honored Russian way present Pat with a gift, this time flowers. Apparently an uneven number of blooms bring good fortune, whereas even numbers are reserved for funerals, but I'm too apprehensive to check! Alexander Nevsky is a gentle giant of a man with a resounding bass voice. "When you meet Nevsky," a newspaper article explains, "and match his congenial personality and caring demeanor with his 6-foot-6, 300-pound frame, it is easy to see why he is so popular." I'm sure he would have cowed even Peter the Great, a man as lofty of stature as he was of reputation. Will our Alexander be able to command his troops as effectively as his historical namesake?

Alexander Izotov—or Sasha, as he prefers—is smaller. A former wrestling champion, he has a smile equally as engaging as his partner's. We are whisked off in the white limo to an Uzbek restaurant, replete with costumed waiters and belly dancers who perform between courses on a smoke-filled, balalaika-throbbing stage. Despite the distractions, we manage to talk—at least Alexander does. Sasha declares that he can only speak English if drunk and proceeds to ensure this genial means of communication.

Like President Putin, Alexander is a nondrinker, the antithesis of one of the Russian stereotypes that his film is attempting to redress. He reminds me that we have already met at a press conference for the last Austin Powers film, when, wearing his Hollywood Foreign Press Association hat, he asked me a question. We learn more details of his antisteroid campaign and discuss the recent announcement by Arnold Schwarzenegger that he is running for the governorship of California in the upcoming special election. Apparently it was seeing him at a recent Golden Globes ceremony that motivated the two friends to think of making this movie. It was also Arnold who inspired their earlier collaboration, *Target Universe,* a TV documentary about bodybuilding that established Alexander as a national star.

As bejeweled bellies shake and shimmy over the shashlik, we talk about the state of contemporary Russian cinema, especially how it has suffered a certain collapse along with the old ideology. The Russians are self-confessed movie fanatics and twenty years ago had one of the world's highest attendance rates, with twenty annual visits per person. Now it has slipped to fewer than two. Soviet cinema, which tended to edify as much as entertain, especially in the golden years of the Mosfilm studios, was followed by a lost decade of imitation Hollywood films that relentlessly exploited previously taboo subjects. As films became fewer, actors—some of them major stars—did television to stay alive. Now there's a return to a cinema that reflects the improved circumstances and Russia's more open society. In the past five years, box office returns have revived at a phenomenal rate.

Nikita Mikhalkov's 1994 Academy Award–winning *Burnt by the Sun* was a powerful examination of the old system and its inbuilt destructive tendencies. On our last visit, Pat and I had the pleasure of lunching with its brilliant screenwriter, the genial Rustam Ibragimbekov, in the House of Writers underneath its spreading chandelier donated by that ruthless editor in chief, Stalin.

Another recent film that particularly impressed was Sergei Bodrov's *Prisoner of the Caucasus,* which unsparingly depicted the effects of the Chechen war, or indeed any war. We saw the film in Sochi, where one of its stars, Oleg Menchikov, confessed to us that his generation had been terrified of the West. We remarked how conditioned we had been to think of the Soviet Union in the same way. Particularly memorable was the eve of the Cuban missile crisis when, as a student at Oxford, I had ordered last drinks in a pub, thinking that they could quite literally be the last we would ever enjoy.

Maybe film, which crosses borders with relative ease and looks as much into the heart as the mind, really can promote awareness with understanding. Both Alexanders consider *Moscow Heat*—not only the biggest independent yet financed in Russia, but the first in English—an important step in the new direction. Hollywood movies tend to recycle unattractive Russian stereotypes such as gangsters, drunken astronauts, or mail-order brides. After so much negativity, having an uncorrupted cop as our hero is a welcome change, although his antagonists will perforce remain the same old-style mobsters and villains. Nonetheless, our producers proudly claim that it will be the first movie in English to portray a Russian action hero and hope it will reflect this astonishing new era as the nation moves toward stability and prosperity.

Like so many of his young contemporaries for whom rents are prohibitive, Alexander is staying with his mother. While here, he wants to spend as much time with her as possible, even though he and his wife, Katya, have their own apartment elsewhere. His mother has all his reviews displayed on a wall, including a negative one to which she draws his attention whenever he threatens to get too big for his already sizable boots. We get to bed late after an enjoyable and enlightening evening, hoping there will be no nocturnal, internal belly dancing from the spicy Uzbek food.

At seven the next morning, splashing through huge puddles, I'm driven through the rainy, gray suburbs for an early morning interview at the Ostankino television center. We pass rush hour buses emblazoned with colorful advertisements for *Pirates of the Caribbean* that look even more out of place in the pervading gloom. Ostankino's lofty concrete mast, like a space ship thrusting through the airwaves, was for ten years the world's tallest tower, and it is still the highest man-made structure in Europe. The sheer bulk of it seems to have leached all the electricity from the rest of the building, leaving it feebly illuminated by low-watt bulbs. Unlike its showbizzy U.S. counterparts, there are no airbrushed smiling photographs or glamorous posters lining the walls, and some distinctly unglamorous soldiers operate the security checkpoint. In sharp contrast, the classically elegant Ostankino palace lies close by in its spacious park, framed by the modern monorail line.

The show is the Russian equivalent of *Good Morning America*, with an audience of 50 million viewers. Few of the country's TV stations, it seems, are now truly independent. Many that were have been shut down or pressured to toe the new Putin line. I'd heard that one of the most popular news channels featured an entirely naked blonde reading the day's events. Has she survived the current changes, I wonder, or has she been thrown her clothes and sent packing?

Meeting up with the Alexanders and Jeff, I'm introduced to our cinematographer, John Aronson, a genial man with alert eyes and an amused smile. In the makeup room my face is painted to a corpselike pallor that, not wishing to hurt international sensibilities, I discreetly wipe away. Our interview, interpreted by a nervous young man from Kazakhstan, lasts ten minutes, in which time we all try to promote our venture with the kind of optimism that all filmmakers have at the outset. François Truffaut, in his magical film *Day for Night,* compared this state to the start of a journey embarked on with the greatest enthusiasm, where you looked forward to the views ahead and to the company. But by the end of it, after all the detours and holdups, the roadblocks and potholes, you just hope to arrive in one piece!

Back in the city center, Pat and I decide to try the Internet café over the road from the National, deep in the bowels of the lavish Okhotny Ryad shopping center at the base of the Kremlin walls. But the café is dark and crowded and full of young American missionaries who, anxious to spread the word in every sense, helpfully explain the new electronic gospel. My e-mail is agonizingly slow and polluted with that devilish new torment, spam, and I give up in disgust. I can't be too upset with the Internet, however, as I hear that in Russia it is providing a vital nexus for open communication, rather like the underground samizdat publications of a previous generation. This becomes especially important as press freedom is increasingly threatened.

That afternoon, we walk west to the Pushkin Fine Arts Museum, with its classical porticoes. A lady at the coat check recognizes me, insisting that we come in for free—another charming bonus, as foreigners generally have to pay a higher entrance fee than the natives. The House of Photography is apparently the lone exception, its director citing the fact that museums in other countries do not practice this double standard. Perhaps this extra tourist income is necessary here, especially as Somerset Maugham maintained, "I can't think of a single Russian novel in which one of the characters goes to a picture gallery."

Again, we are overwhelmed by the diversity of the artworks, which include a huge collection of French impressionist paintings, as well as antique sculptures. In addition, there's *I Love Petersburg,* a special exhibition celebrating that city's three-hundredth anniversary. It's somewhat ironic, though, that many other works from St. Petersburg's State Russian Museum are currently being displayed back home in Los Angeles. There is also, of all things, a quirky little show of sculptures by Gina Lollobrigida.

Walking back in the traffic fumes, we dodge the racing vehicles by bolting for safety into pedestrian tunnels. The car is definitely czar here, and there seem to be more of them every day. Apparently there is a particular crossing over one of the ring roads that can require as much as a fifteen-minute wait, calling on every iota of fatalistic patience bred by the old system. At present, for every 1,000 inhabitants, there are 160 cars, but this is predicted to leap soon to 250 per 1,000. As in Paris in the rebellious 1970s, vehicles are frequently parked at random on the sidewalks, like steel flotsam. The energetic mayor, Yuri Luzhkov, tried to introduce London taxicabs, but as in New York, the roads proved too inhospitable for such sedate carriages.

Back in the hotel, the official Moscow tourist guide provides "a piece of advice for travelers." Among an itemized list is the essential warning that "cars are not obliged to stop at pedestrian crossings to allow pedestrians to cross." It also urges, "Don't walk alone at night" and, "Try to avoid using the public transport if you have a large sum of money with you." Persisting with this financial theme, it counsels, "Don't use the services of Russian prostitutes, otherwise you can lose your money." Some might consider this loss worthwhile, for Moscow's ladies of the night—at least from discreet observation—seem especially beautiful.

Czar Pictures has delivered a cell phone. Now they can keep tabs on me at all hours. It's an electronic ball and chain with no escape. No more civilized messages slipped silently under the door, no more soundproof booths. I join the swelling ranks of the peace disturbers, like the miscreant who interrupted my performance in Stockholm with his churlish clanging. One of my favorite objects, acquired at a Moscow gallery on our previous visit and increasingly enjoyed for its symbolic value, is a perfectly carved wooden mobile phone.

That evening we dine again at the Café Pushkin as another downpour soaks the city. Feeling lucky to get a table in the packed, lively place, we are even more fortunate to get a cab back to the hotel through the deluge—even when $15 is demanded for the short ride. A sheepish Robert Madrid told me that, unaware of the proximity of his hotel, he was once fleeced of $30 for the three-block trip. But having heard that as much as $200 can be charged to the airport, I hand over the rubles with only a token protest. Capitalism!

It prompts memories of the time we were in St. Petersburg during White Nights, that enchanting summer season when, in that northerly latitude, the sun never entirely sets, and longed to take a boat out on the Neva River to enjoy the unearthly, sepulchral midnight light. But many others had the same idea, and there were long queues. Notwithstanding, our Russian host blithely went to the head of one and negotiated with the boatman amid howls of protest from the patient ranks of waiting tourists. Turning to them, he explained with excessive politeness that in Russia there had been a switch from a Communist to a capitalist economy. He was now merely practicing a fundamental capitalistic technique: offering more money for the privilege of special service. Before the dumbfounded onlookers could react, we were shadows in the silvery distance!

The rain turns out to be of record proportions—nearly as much in one day as is usual for the entire month—and the Metro, Moscow's famous subway system, is flooded. Meanwhile, in France, three thousand people die of the heat. Russians seem more fixated on the weather than most other nations; forecasts even include reports of sunspot activity, reputed to cause all manner of ailments. Such spots are distinctly absent the next morning as the limo conveys us through the persistent drizzle to the southeastern fringes of Moscow. When we snap on our seat belts, the driver anxiously inquires if his conduct is making us nervous. Incurably independent, I usually rent a car when on location and take pleasure in driving myself. This makes for interesting, unexpected encounters, and Pat and I have shared much from the front seat of a moving vehicle. Now, with so many unfamiliar, unreadable traffic signs, I'm happy to be seated in the back.

Suddenly, beyond the last tram stop, lakes appear amid trees and, crossing a castellated bridge, we arrive at the Tsaritsino Palace. Many of the film's fight sequences will be staged here, and in the first few days of shooting, it will also stand in for the campus of a U.S. college. It's a strange, ghostly place—at the same time both unfinished and ruined—and looks chillingly uninviting in the damp, fresh air. I have an eerie feeling that other duels, many of them deadly, have been held here before.

An amalgam of red bricks and white stone patchworked in a strange, pseudo-Gothic style, the palace complex was begun by Catherine the Great, only to be abandoned ten years later after a dispute with her architect. In a fit of pique, she even tried to pull it down, just as she had attempted to destroy and rebuild Moscow's ancient Kremlin. Fortunately the money ran out, allowing this monument to extravagance and whim to survive. Like so many other buildings in Russia, it is now being restored, with part of it being used as a museum that houses a small collection of icons and photographs.

That afternoon we drive past exciting contemporary examples of that same bold architectural heritage that is reshaping Moscow. There's a sense of looking into the future, as with the present radical transformation of Shanghai or Berlin. A brand-new glass and steel concert hall seems to have landed by the river like a glittering space ship. Some of this development is controversial. To accommodate it, over one hundred historic buildings have been razed, constituting the most drastic reconstruction of the city since the Brezhnev era. Their replacements have been denigrated in some quarters as a "malignant tumor" on the landscape.

That could also be said of the aging Modern Tretyakov gallery, which seems nothing more than a dull concrete monument to the blank, airport-terminal style of Soviet architecture. On its roof a huge, incongruously surreal Lipton's Tea sign that only Andy Warhol could love renders the surly pile absurd—the same effect made by a pigeon squatting on the head of some pompous statue. Inside, we start to feel exhausted, although walls full of lively Exters and Goncharovas revive flagging spirits. The gallery mostly displays Russian works with scant reflection of the international ferment in art. Moreover, there seems little enthusiasm for showing contemporary art—and this is the country that gave birth to Kasimir Malevich's revolutionary black square. Such displays are left to the new commercial galleries.

Back at the hotel there are further costume fittings—including a tight but natty fencing outfit. Here we go again, once more unto the breeches—en garde! That evening we meet the two Alexanders for drinks and pastries in the glass-paneled coffee shop. There's further discussion about the script, and both are encouraged to hold out for their vision of a film that more accurately and interestingly reflects the realities of their new Russia, rather than trotting out the same outmoded and formulaic Western clichés.

Trying to fix more about my character, the still elusive Roger Chambers, I ask if he is a U.S. resident or just there to visit his son? Or both? My preference is for him to be retired in LA, and I offer to do a day's guerrilla filming there to establish this in our film's opening credits. This tallies with their concept of Roger as a man existing somewhat outside the mainstream of American life, and they like my suggestion of him at first refusing to be armed. We comment on a report in today's paper paralleling a theme of our script about the first-time cooperation between U.S. and Russian security forces.

We spend Friday morning revisiting the Kremlin, the heart of Moscow and of the country, and a city within the city. Our guide Olga, flaxen of hair and fluent of English, is an ideal blend of intelligence and information, with a pleasant voice. Her previous clients, she tells us, have included Malcolm Forbes—no doubt when he was here buying up all those Fabergé eggs. Being obliged to spend time with strangers serving as interpreters puts a great significance on their personalities. We have been extraordinarily lucky on our past few visits, having been placed in the elegant, educated hands of Viktoria Melnick, who became a good friend. We toured the city with her, enjoying her many interesting and amusing insights. I especially remember her pointing out the Kremlin guide who never told the same story twice about objects on display—presumably to keep himself as entertained as his audience.

We were later delighted to find an unusual way to repay Viktoria's many kindnesses. Once, when working on an Anglo-Russian theatrical venture, she joined us at a Moscow Film Festival dinner, where she expressed an attraction to a certain French filmmaker, Jean-Louis Leconte, seated nearby. Pat ascertained that he felt similar stirrings for Viktoria. In flagrant *Hello Dolly* mode, my matchmaking wife then made sure that each constantly, involuntarily spent time with the other. The outcome was a phone call from Paris three months later announcing their wedding, followed eventually by a joyful note reporting the birth of their son.

The Kremlin is invaded by hordes of visitors but seemingly few Americans, even though the Russian tourist industry is growing by roughly 10 percent a year. With Olga, queues are jumped or at least curtailed—except those inevitably long ones inside for the *tualet*—and we gain the fast track into this extraordinary amalgam of fortress and treasure house. What the Russian church inherited from Byzantium is everywhere in evidence, from the domed exteriors to gilded gloom of the icon-filled interiors. A story has it that Russia considered Islam and Judaism before converting to Orthodox Christianity. In the upshot, both faiths were rejected because it seemed unlikely that Russians would embrace a religion that discouraged the use of alcohol!

We are swamped by the sheer sumptuousness of it all and dizzy with the ambient opulence, particularly admiring the exquisite Fabergé pieces that Mr. Forbes seems to have overlooked. I was reminded of a memorable visit with President Richard Nixon in San Clemente just after his ignominious departure from high office. He showed us the modest bedroom where Premier Leonid Brezhnev had stayed and, in strong contrast, photographs of the prerevolutionary splendor in which he himself had been enveloped on his Russian visit.

We had marveled at the Kremlin's panoply of jewels, crowns, furs, and king's ransoms on previous visits, but for the first time we visit the Diamond Fund Exhibition, a dimly lit Ali Baba's cave of dazzling gems that provide its main illumination and allure. What is it about jewels that drives the human imagination to excess? Apparently it was not unusual in Communist times for the wives and daughters of the country's elite to visit the Diamond Fund and pick out a priceless trinket for their own use, often on a permanent basis.

Not unsurprisingly for one so given to extravagant excess, among the biggest gems are those owned by Catherine the Great. She was an inveterate collector of precious things as well as men, amassing more art in thirty years than the Louvre managed to assemble in four hundred. On display is a particularly huge rock of a diamond given to her by one of her lovers. It prompts recollection of a story about Mae West who, impersonating the legendary monarch in a Broadway play called *Catherine Was Great,* ad-libbed to her lover the immortal line, "Is that your sword or are you just pleased to see me?" Reviewing her performance, one critic sneered: "Mae West slips up on the steppes," to which she gamely retorted, "Catherine had three hundred lovers. I did the best I could in a couple of hours!"

The sheer profligate excess of the exhibition induces the same reaction experienced when visiting other sumptuous repositories of incalculable wealth, such as the Vatican. Surely the imprisoned riches would better serve those who patiently line up to goggle if they were sold off and used for meaningful pensions and other social amelioration. But these treasure troves are obviously a source of great national pride as well as tourist revenue. It helps explain why further king's ransoms are being expended on regilding everything, even to the extent of recreating St. Petersburg's fabled Amber Room, stolen and presumed lost in World War II.

For a country that was once officially atheist, the Kremlin has a surprising number of religious buildings. One square alone houses the Cathedral of the Dormition, the Cathedral of the Annunciation, and the Cathedral of the Archangel. In Soviet times the Kremlin served as a powerful paradigm for the walling up of religion. At the same time, the ruling elite transmogrified Christian iconography as astutely as the early Christians had appropriated pagan symbols and festivals—even the May Day display of politicians atop Lenin's tomb, with the leader in the center surrounded by his acolytes, was a subliminal secular duplication of the imagery of the Last Supper.

Feeling like extras in an opulent performance of *Boris Godunov,* we take in the extravagant scene that includes the world's biggest bell. Never rung and now broken, it is presumably yet another candidate for the current refurbishment. A profusion of palaces ennobles every prospect. It is difficult to associate such colorful and playful architecture with the grim orders for political purges and Cold War killings that must have emanated from within. Sundry other towers and belfries mark the centuries of construction as well as toll the more recent hours. By the time midday strikes, our eyes and feet are worn out, and we politely decline Olga's energetic offer to tour those other opulent palaces, the Metro stations.

A sudden downpour thwarts our planned afternoon on the river, driving us into the vaulted, multileveled building on Red Square with a name as imposing as its huge dimensions: Gosudarstvenniy Universalny Magazin or, less pompously, GUM. The huge emporium, glimpsed in the background of so many Soviet parades, has been transformed into another sort of Ali Baba's cave—a Kremlin of consumerism housing opulent fashion aristocrats alongside humble kiosks peddling matryoshka dolls.

At the end of the nineteenth century, the city was "Calico Moscow," a great textile center, and is now reverting to its rag trade preeminence. Although today there's not much cloth in evidence:

garments seem fashionably minimalist. I'm reminded of a trip to Paris earlier in the year when all the outfits in the couturiers' windows seemed uncharacteristically brief and trashy. It was explained that an important clientele consisted of Russian prostitutes, their tastes and cash payments dictating prevailing trends. This is all a far cry from the time when the Soviet House of Patterns, the central fashion organization, designed clothes for the people, employing size XXL models whose retirement age was a geriatric seventy-eight. For men there was little choice other than polyester suits and tracksuits. Jeans and low necklines were banned as part of a Canute-like effort to stem the tide of Western corruption.

Outside, the same colorful rainbow hovers obsequiously over Lenin's roseate tomb as we return to the hotel. There we encounter my "son," Adrian Paul—minus his luggage, lost by the airline in the latest Great New York Electrical Blackout. Having returned from buying replacement clothes, he's now anxious to get to work on the script and, after showering and shaving, comes to our suite for tea. Adrian seems intense and motivated. He has even spent time in the field with the Los Angeles Police Department to authenticate his role as a young officer moved to join the force by the death of his mother in a terrorist attack.

Toward 11:00 P.M., a time when I'm usually thinking more of bed than of banqueting, we are all invited by our producers to dinner at one of Moscow's latest neon nightclubs, a glass-and-chrome palace of hedonism that astonishes with its luxurious opulence. Outside a phalanx of black-leather-jacketed bodyguards awaits, and within there are courtyards and balconies, all accessed by huge glass elevators and embellished by trendily underclad girls. This must be part of the "round the clock revelry" promised by the Moscow tourist guide.

Much as I appreciate our hosts' hospitality and the pleasure of informally initiating our venture, I find myself reacting in an

almost puritanical way to the lateness of the hour and the elabo-
rateness of the meal. Wanting to preserve my energy for the filming ahead and perhaps also to send a gentle, subliminal message
that I'm here to work, not play, I find an excuse to go home early
with Pat, much as we would love to linger in such a seductive mi-
lieu. My philosophy has always been that, if you give a film 100
percent of your application and talent, then you can walk away
from its outcome with a certain impunity. The fate of any such
enterprise, so fraught with imponderables, is anyway unknow-
able, so doing one's Boy Scout best is the least contribution one
can make.

The next day finds us in a sun-struck Red Square that is alive
with weekend brides and animated with people like an L. S.
Lowry painting. Pat photographs Alexander and myself, and, rec-
ognized by two youths, my co-star also generously poses with
them. When it's my turn, I feel minuscule alongside his bulging,
steroid-free physique. I'm reminded of Noel Coward's famous reply, "That's her lunch," on being asked who was the diminutive
gentleman sitting next to the generously proportioned Queen
Salote of Tonga in the 1953 coronation procession. What a relief
that, in the movie, Alexander and I only battle wits, not fists. His
transformation to his present size is little short of incredible. He
gives Pat a copy of his book that sports a picture of him in his
wimpish, underdeveloped boyhood. Pat trades it for *Going Strong,*
a book of her photographs of people over the age of seventy-five
who, unlike so many of their Russian contemporaries, are still
working full time. On request, she inscribes it to Putin who,
given his ascetic regimen, should be long going strong.

Afterward Pat and I are taken to the studios of Ekho Moskvy, or
Moscow Echo, the city's leading independent radio station, for an
hour-long interview with us both. We notice that a photo taken
on our last visit now adorns the walls of this crowded warren,

along with those of countless other interviewees. There are call-in questions, including a few from farthest Siberia, curious about the new film and our impressions of the changes to Russia. Though uncertain if Moscow's transformation is reflected in the rest of the country, we are genuinely complimentary. I have always enjoyed myself here and say so.

Ignoring the gathering storm clouds menacing the skyline, we embark on that promised Moscow River trip in one of the many sleek vessels plying the waters. I remember doing this somewhat guiltily thirty years ago when I should have been dutifully in-doors watching movies as a guest of the Moscow Film Festival. But our visit coincided with weather of an unblemished perfec-tion that lured us out of the dark, theatrical confines and into the cinema verité of the sunlit streets.

This excursion is well timed. No sooner are we aboard and un-der cover in a cabin crammed with fellow trippers than the skies open and pour out a Noah-esque deluge. Nonetheless it is all very relaxing as we take in the slowly passing sights—the wedding cake of a Kremlin impenetrable behind thick walls; the Red Oc-tober chocolate factory, makers of a fearsomely sweet product; and the long green strip of Gorky Park with the bulky Soviet space shuttle prominently parked by the fun fair. It never left the ground, a fate that should have been shared by Concordski, the doomed challenger to the Anglo-French supersonic airliner.

At one point two giggling teenagers come and sit by us, and for a few flattering moments, I assume it is because of me. But Vlad, our long-haired, eighteen-year-old, T-shirted and be-jeaned minder, quickly disabuses me of this notion. "I look just like a famous Rus-sian pop star," he self-effacingly explains. With a restored sun now gilding everything, we get off upriver near the White House, home of the Russian government where, atop a tank, Boris Yeltsin made his historic, epoch-shaping stand against the hardliners in 1991.

It was also the place where in 1993 the same Yeltsin ordered tanks to fire at the same building. Viktoria Leconte, an eyewitness, described the incident feelingly: "I did not much agree with the opposition which was still inside, but it was really something unbelievable in our modern democratic time to stay on the other part of the bridge with many other spectators and watch the tanks shooting at the parliament of a civilized country, with all of the world watching and nothing to be done."

Next morning I reluctantly return Pat to the airport for her flight to LA. She's taking the only direct one on Aeroflot—a mere twelve and a half hours' hop directly over the North Pole. Much as she would love to stay on longer, the pressures to resume work on her exhibition are growing. Besides, once the film starts, I will not have much of a social life to share. Our ride in the limo, with decanters and glasses tinkling over the bumps, is relatively brief. The traffic-choked drive can take as long as five hours. We have come early, a practice I now insist on after too many white-knuckle airport dashes in the hands of people who wrongly assume they are doing you a favor by delivering you at the very last moment.

Such an incident occurred a few years ago driving to this same airport. We were traveling from the Black Sea resort of Sochi, which involved landing at Moscow's national airport and then taking the long, laborious outer ring road around to Sheremetyevo, the international one. Arriving there late, we joined a long line of passengers waiting to go through the agonizingly slow departure formalities. The last call for our "Luftgansa" flight was made as we inched forward, and then, just as we finally arrived at passport control, a burly Mafia type and his equally overdressed lady pushed in front of us, physically shoving Pat aside. He should have known better than to pick on my wife with such discourtesy. Snatching his proffered passports and hurling them the length of the departure hall, Pat at the same time admonished the astonished onlookers not to tolerate such behavior. Images of a night in jail flashed before me as I tried to restrain her. Mercifully, we were hustled through and onto the plane, which was actually pulling away as we jumped aboard!

My wife is now the model of good behavior as we arrive at the busy airport. Like the privileged *nomenklatura* of the recent past, we are escorted to the VIP room. Unchanged since we last used it, with dark paneling, ineffectual lighting, and the kind of dull rubber plants beloved of eastern European furnishing, it's a waiting room that discourages waiting. It is unfortunate that Soviet-era Sheremetyevo provides the first glimpse of Russia for most visitors. The old mistrustful habit of taking your passport and boarding pass until your flight is called also persists.

Like that final scene in *Casablanca,* Pat eventually bids me farewell, and the lowering clouds, in a bravura display of the pathetic fallacy, begin to weep copiously as I slink back to the car. At the National, our suite reverts to being a bachelor's abode for the next month or so. And that unknown "so" is fraught with weighty significance—can this film really be made in the time allotted, or will I still be here at Christmas?

The hotel coffee shop already betrays a sign that fall is imminent—mushrooms, that immemorial Russian passion, are featured on the menu. Meeting there with Jeff and Tony Leung, our action director from Hong Kong, we discuss the fencing match between Adrian and myself, the first scene to be filmed. Small, lithe, and bursting with ideas, Tony envisions a relatively complicated sequence, whereas I had just imagined a simple, friendly bout between father and son that could be knocked off in a morning's shooting. I'm not sure how appropriate Tony's proposed flying foil display is for the story. Stressing that action is character, I remind him that I'm playing a diplomat and don't want to appear like some superannuated James Bond. At least my character should lose the fencing bout, I suggest, so that his later trouncing of the villainous Nikolay in the saber duel is not a foregone conclusion.

Jeff is slightly at a loss to help because his hotel maids have inadvertently thrown away his script notes, along with other personal and research papers—even checkbooks. The trash has been combed, but to no avail. So we talk lengthily in general, often going in as many circles as the roads around Moscow. A story about John Gielgud slowly impinges on my subconscious. At a rehearsal of Seneca's *Oedipus,* the director, Peter Brook, asked his cast to improvise the most horrifying thing they could envision. Following a series of extravagant emoting from the others, at his turn Sir John said simply, "We open on Tuesday."

Eventually Adrian and I get away to my room and, in a few minutes, rewrite our first scene. Ah, the joys of working with an English actor whose instinct is more to quickly show than elaborately tell. That evening I go for a swim in a gilded pool and reflect that Pat, flying into the very same endless sunset, still has a quarter of her journey to complete. Ordering room service, that chief prize of hotel living other than free shoe shines, I reflect further on the character, so shadowy and indefinite on paper, that I am about to commit to celluloid.

Ultimately, a film role only comes to life when imagination, as much as slavish research, is the main motivator. I have impersonated politicians before—a whole United Nations full of them—and have met many and known a few. I remember the chilling atmosphere of formal unease surrounding Franjo Tudjman, the former president of Croatia, when he received Pat and me in his Zagreb palace, and conversely how relaxed the former most powerful man in the world, Bill Clinton, could be. I have had the pleasure of knowing many British ambassadors in Washington and their consular colleagues in Los Angeles. During the first Gulf War, in a last hurrah for the old Empire glory, I was even telephoned by Her Majesty's consul to Israel, where I had been filming. Even as my fellow cast members, similarly contacted by their respective embassies, were flying from the threatened country, he proudly informed me that arrangements had been made for a gunboat to evacuate British nationals from Eilat! Damn fine show, what?

I'm on my own—a condition that, since boyhood, I have always preferred when the company of loved ones or special friends was unavailable.

PART TWO

Action?

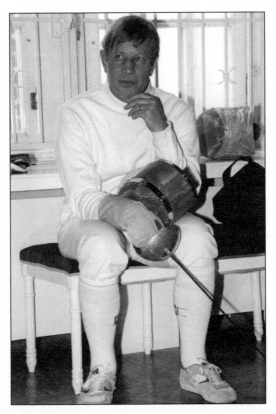

Well, *are* my blinkers showing?

Три · 3

Hurry Up and Wait

Everything is funny as long as it happens to someone else.

— RUSSIAN PROVERB

Today's scheduled filming has been postponed until tomorrow. At least this delay will allow us to spend the time rehearsing—always an invaluable luxury and a real investment.

Adrian joins me at breakfast, and we further revise our scene so that it now reveals much information—our "back story," or mutual history before the film's start—but gives it away incidentally. Adrian types it up at the Business Center, this brief activity setting us back $14—a very good business! I ask the young lady in attendance—only half jokingly—how anyone can possibly afford to live here now, and she responds unsmilingly with a fateful shrug.

There's an e-mail waiting from Pat. Her flight was apparently agreeable, especially the generous helpings of caviar. The only drawback was the equally generous line to get through U.S. immigration—according to one porter, a wait of three hours was not unusual in these nervous new times. Superpower America now seems to have inherited its old Soviet rival's legendary queues.

Sasha Izotov invites Adrian and me to another themed restaurant for a lunch served by flaxen-plaited "peasants." They give us *kvas*, fermented rye water, which is very refreshing, if a little intoxicating. Apparently the *kvas* truck used to be as familiar as the ice cream cart is today. I also discover a delicious Georgian sparkling mineral water called Borjomi and wonder if some day soon it will be a rival to the all-pervasive Perrier.

Back at Tsaritsino, our American first assistant director, Whitney Hunter, is introduced. His is one of the most important jobs on the movie. The great enabler and organizer, he is often required to think fast on his feet to counter the emergencies that inevitably materialize despite all the careful preparation. Deceptively mild-mannered, Whitney has made six films in Russia and would seem a perfect choice for this cross-cultural venture.

Wearing huge felt booties to protect the antique floor, we rehearse the fencing bout and ensuing dialogue. I flash back to the 1970s and visiting Tolstoy's country birthplace at Yasnaya Polyana, where all the shuffling overshoes lent the mansion an appropriate hushed reverence as well as a lustrous shine. The younger, pre-sage Tolstoy would presumably have approved of our present martial activity—and the violent overtones of our film's plot—having revealed in *A Confession* that he had "challenged men to duels with the purpose of killing them."

Tony Leung is a whirl of ideas and actions, all expressed in wonderfully approximate English. His fight choreography is interesting to behold, though I'm still concerned about the appropriateness of some of the Hong Kong–style action for my character. Tony enthuses about bursting balloons and slicing through candles in the best swashbuckler style, of which I retain both imperishable memories and not a few scars.

Tomorrow's expected call sheet—the listed requirements for the day's filming—doesn't arrive until just before midnight, and so I'm abed later than intended. Wanting to be in optimum shape for the morrow, I know from experience that sleep will not come easily. I think back on other movies where well-meaning producers liked to entertain their casts before the first day of filming. The night before *Logan's Run* took its first step, I longed to run from the noisy Dallas restaurant where I reluctantly found myself, listening only to next morning's dialogue racing neurotically through my antisocial head. I suppose it's best called stage fright, and it never goes away.

Tuesday, August 19: the first day of filming! An energy of anticipation enlivens everything. A headline in the newspaper reads, "Arms market a menace to the entire world," which seems a propitious omen for the start of this film. Leaving early in the pouring rain for Tsaritsino, on arrival I'm ushered into a huge trailer. There is even a stewardess in attendance, fetchingly dressed in a white shirt and trim black skirt, who introduces herself as Svetlana. She immediately makes tea—another good omen!

However, the trailer eventually becomes a little too public, with much noisy coming and going, and I ask if I can use a smaller, more private one. Trailers may seem like an indulgence—some of today's stars seem to rank their importance by the relative size of their quarters—but a place not just for changing clothes is essential. Films are rarely rehearsed, so they provide an indispensable refuge where one can learn, plot, and think in peace away from the endless distractions on set. My request is initially denied—the best has been reserved for me. However, there is eventually and fortuitously an overpowering smell of gas, and when I start to feel giddy, my wish is granted. In the smaller, quieter, and more intimate setting, I'm served by a young man called Nazar, formally dressed like Svetlana in natty black and white.

After more time and an indecent amount of tea, I inquire why nothing much seems to be happening. Apparently the camera is stuck in a traffic jam. Forcing myself to be Zen-like, I go for a walk in the sunshine that now graces the scene and then run through lines with Robert Madrid. Finally, well past midday, the camera truck arrives. Before we start, however, there is another delay, occasioned this time by a little ceremony. Reminding me of filming in India, where the camera is first garlanded like the deity it is, a commemorative plate is broken, like the symbolic smashed glass at a Jewish wedding. We toast the success of our mixed marriage of talents, intentions, and nationalities.

The very first shot is of Robert and me walking down a long avenue, talking about the death of a beloved son and colleague. At its conclusion, I vow to accompany Robert to Moscow to help track down the killers. It's unusual to begin at the beginning; it's more customary to start in the middle or the end. This lack of sequentiality never bothers me as it seems more reflective of real life, with its unpredictable mood swings and inconsistencies. It also ensures that the entire script, not just the scenes for the day, is well prepared in advance. I still find the process of acting immensely enjoyable: the opportunity to create a complex, multifaceted character that will both serve the written script and, hopefully, embellish it. This, perhaps, is nothing more than a long-term evolution of those childish games of make-believe.

Today happens to be a holiday, and a curious and very noisy crowd fills the scene. Many walk through the shot despite the pleas of our several still uncoordinated Russian assistant directors, who run around frantically responding to a continual feed of information into their earpieces like demented Secret Service agents. Work is constantly interrupted by peals of bells as well as jolly music from a nearby fun fair. Moreover, the pretty little estate church we had hoped to use for the funeral scene is now being employed for its proper purpose. Robert and I both wear radio microphones, but even with the added proximity of regular boomed mikes, much of the sound is compromised. Finally, we finish at about three in the afternoon, and I retire to a lunch served by Nazar on elegant china plates. Adrian joins me so that we can rehearse at the same time—and get a feel for the relationship we are about to depict.

This conversation is to be filmed outside on the steps of the museum that, with appropriate signage, is standing in for the American campus. By now a huge, talkative audience has gathered in front of us, including many members of the press eager for interviews and photo opportunities. There is even a crew filming the filming for later promotional purposes. It's all rather distracting, but it seems churlish to complain, especially as the scene plays well. Like the grit in the oyster, problems often produce pearls. When the light eventually fades, the company retires inside to start immortalizing the fencing match.

We have the museum to ourselves, but all the treading-on-eggshells caution of the previous day appears to have vanished. Why do people tend to lower their defenses for film crews? Why is cinema such an "open sesame"? Why don't more people echo the exasperatedly polite plea, "It would be so nice if you weren't here," made by an upper-class English lady to Charles Grodin and Candice Bergen when they were filming in her grand house? Our initial request to film in the museum was apparently turned down as "impossible"—and yet here we are, taking over the place like invading Cossacks.

The loss of time has forced Tony to simplify his choreography—a plus, as far as I am concerned, although many bravura moves remain. Since the impenetrable fencing masks make Adrian and me indistinguishable, I gratefully allow a lithe young stuntman to double me, reaping all of his athletic glory. Adrian characteristically prefers to do his own work. Nonetheless, we both return home exhausted toward midnight. I phone Pat to report that finally film has run through the camera.

The journalists have been busy overnight. There's an article in the morning paper about our movie under the headline "Alexander Nevsky pumps up the 'Heat.'" I learn a great deal, including the fact that our film has received organizational and logistical support from city authorities, specifically Deputy Mayor Valery Shantsev, and from GUBOP, the Interior Ministry's organized crime department. "My character is a GUBOP officer," Alexander is quoted as saying, "so we asked the head of the unit, Valery Ovchinnikov, to help out to make sure everything would be realistic."

Today Adrian's death scene is being filmed, so I'm not needed. It's a beautiful morning with a cloudless blue sky: perfect for a walk in Gorky Park, the title and setting of one of our co-star Joanna Pacula's most eminent films—even though it was actually made in Helsinki. Giving my bodyguard the slip—like Greta Garbo's Grusinskaya in *Grand Hotel,* I want to be alone—I set out along the riverbank, passing the huge (some would say kitschy) modern statue of Peter the Great that seems to have strayed from the Muscovite equivalent of Disneyland. It appears about to whirr, salute, and tinnily sing some imperial anthem while steel flags unfurl and mechanically flap. The story has it that this metallic behemoth originally depicted Christopher Columbus, but, rejected by every prospective American city, it was conveniently transformed into this other legendary admiral. How ironic that Peter, who despised Moscow to the extent of creating a new capital in St. Petersburg, should be so prominently commemorated here.

Gorky Park is full of pleasure seekers. Slim young girls with the internationally mandated bare midriff mingle with visitors from the provinces with their old-fashioned clothes and overdyed hair, while children enjoy roller coaster rides and pedalos on the lake.

Numerous bars and cafés enliven the landscape with bright plastic furniture, each blaring its own lively pop song and creating a pleasant cacophony. I sit and read the paper, enjoying the sunshine, the ambient relaxed mood, and the sense of freedom—mine as much as the residents'. This week commemorates the anniversary of the 1991 counterrevolution. In Bratislava at the time on a movie, we witnessed the world-weary Slovaks resign themselves to seeing Soviet tanks returning to the city. Coincidentally, there's an article in the morning paper lauding the cosmopolitan charms of today's independent Bratislava.

Just outside the amusement park there is a chilling historical reminder—a sculpture park where many monumental statues of former Communist leaders have found an ingloriously lowly and crowded resting place. Stalins are cheek-by-jowl with Lenins, their fallen hammers and sickles liberally littering the ground. Further along, there is a moving monument to the victims of these tyrants, making even more controversial a proposal to restore some of the fallen idols to their empty plinths.

In the evening I'm invited out by an American currently resident in Moscow. There's something rather louche and predatory about him—apparently Moscow is now full of similar opportunists. Claiming he wants to discuss a film project, he lures me to the Vogue Café, the ultimate in contemporary trendiness. You had to pinch yourself that you had not just walked off the streets of London, Paris, or New York. The choice of restaurants in Moscow is becoming as diverse as in any other major city: twenty new establishments open every month. This one is owned by Arkady Novikov, described as the Russian Wolfgang Puck, whom I then have the pleasure of meeting. He owns more than fifty of the city's other restaurants—all of them social hubs.

A beautifully dressed lady waves and sends over a red rose with a note that reveals her to be the distinguished designer Helen

Yarmak. At an adjoining table sits an equally impeccably dressed man, gold cufflinks winking out of a well-cut suit, who turns out to be Petr Aven. Owning banks and TV stations, he is one of the now legendary oligarchs who dominate the country's business. In the late 1980s a dozen of them controlled half the economy, having gobbled up the assets in the free-for-all that followed President Yeltsin's privatization of the sclerotic Soviet command economy— a time when even Yeltsin himself described his chaotic country as a "Mafia state." Now Russia boasts several dozen billionaires, mostly in their thirties. One of them, Roman Abramovich, is the world's richest man under forty. Their combined wealth is equal to an astonishing quarter of the country's gross domestic product. The *Art* newspaper reports that in 2000 *Forbes* magazine had not a single Russian on its list of the world's richest people. Now only America, Germany, and Japan boast more billionaires.

I'm delighted when Petr invites me to join him for a drink because I'm curious to find out more from the source about this controversial clique. My carpetbagging host, who has already tried to maneuver me into picking up the check, is impressed, no doubt sniffing fresh opportunities. Petr and I talk at length about Gollywood, as well as the new Russia he is helping create. There has been a sort of economic miracle since 1999, fueled by high oil prices and an annual growth rate of more than 5 percent, making Russia's the best performing major economy after China. Foreign investment is rising, and Russian stocks are among the best performing of the emergent markets. Putin and his *siloviki*—men of power—have anchored this prosperity with a new stability and predictability under the president's "dictatorship of the law." All this is in strong contrast to the waning days of the ailing Soviet Union, when Mikhail Gorbachev was the fourth leader in as many years.

Sitting with Petr is the deputy governor of a Siberian province who waxes eloquent on its pristine beauties and immense, untapped riches. What a different connotation Siberia now has, compared to those bleak totalitarian days when it represented the last stop on the exile's long, one-way trip to the gulag. Both men are horrified to learn that I was in Gorky Park without a bodyguard, but after the post-9/11 paranoia permeating American society today, I assure them that Russia doesn't seem so dangerous a place.

Back in the hotel lobby, I encounter an old acquaintance, Andrea Andermann, the Italian producer, here to discuss possible co-productions. Andrea was responsible for the recent sumptuous *La Traviata*, televised live from Paris around the world, and I immediately visualize a future *Boris Godunov* booming from the Kremlin. He mentions the need to be firm and authoritative in dealing with Russians—"In bocca di lupa," the Italian equivalent of "break a leg," is his parting imprecation. I fleetingly contemplate spitting three times over my left shoulder, the local way of warding off misfortune.

Another cast member, Richard Tyson, arrives from California. With his brooding, taciturn presence, he will be playing the film's chief villain, the Russian American gangster Nikolay. At breakfast, seeing a young baby being fed at the next table, he suffers immediate pangs of homesickness, having just kissed his own five-month-old daughter good-bye. Enforced family separation is one of the concomitant penalties of moviemaking. We discuss our film, especially about eliminating any clichés that might still cling to the characters. But as his role could at times be seen to exemplify that description, I don't press the issue.

It's raining again, and I'm happy to be indoors in the hotel coffee shop being interviewed by a young lady journalist. A photographer clicks relentlessly away throughout the session, mostly at floor level. I dread seeing the results, as Pat has advised me to always request being shot from the more flattering above rather than the distorting below. Trying to turn the tables on my interlocutor, I ask questions about life in these new times. I can't help thinking of the attractive girl who interviewed me a few years ago in St. Petersburg. Pat was then working on a series where she photographed people going about their ordinary business at work, but naked. Astonishingly, over 80 percent of those asked agreed to pose, as happened with this girl, who had no qualms about stripping down to a bare microphone. How different from Soviet times, when erotic art was discouraged, Stalin even sending one offender, the brilliant photographer Alexander Grinberg, to a labor camp for transgressing his fig-leafed standards.

My stomach being upset, I go out in search of a vegetarian restaurant that's been recommended. Though providing a diverting stroll, my quarry proves elusive, so I buy some apples from a street market. As I head back, my guts are further wrenched when I pass the building where the Lubyanka prison, the headquarters of the KGB, was once situated. Incarcerated indoors that afternoon, I spend it reading scripts as rain scours a gloomy Red Square.

Actors, as much as traveling salesmen, inevitably become connoisseurs of hotel life, especially hotel rooms. Pat and I often fantasize about being commissioned to design the ideal room. This would be not so much a question of luxury as of practicality— the availability of simple hooks to hang, and shelves to hold, essentials. Hotel designers obviously never indulge in that true luxury, reading in bed, as lights are invariably dim or ill placed. And it is axiomatic that all hotel safes will have pitch-black interiors, guaranteeing that the departing guest leaves behind some bounty as an involuntary tip.

Perhaps hiding valuables under the mattress is still the safest means of securing them. I remember a heart-stopping moment in an Indian hotel. After noticing a sign disclaiming any responsibility for valuables unless they were placed in the hotel safe, we gathered our passports and other treasures into a bag and asked the receptionist to secure them as recommended. Just before our departure, I went to reclaim them, only to be told that our bag was not in the safe. Describing the man to whom it had been entrusted, I insisted on speaking to him. "Not possible, sir. He is now sleeping." "Well, get him," I almost shouted. Eventually the aroused individual arrived by bicycle, seeming most upset that we should be upset. Going to an unlocked broom closet in the lobby, he calmly produced the missing bag that had been in full view of the busy hotel's comings and goings for days.

That evening finds me back at Ostankino, which looks even more gloomy and underlit in the dark. I'm there for another national TV show to be broadcast early tomorrow. In fact, it is going live to Vladivostok as it's already morning there, giving some indication of Russia's breadth, one-sixth of the world's landmass, stretched over eleven time zones and containing one hundred ethnic groups. The makeup girl provides tea and cakes as well as facial embellishment. The show uses the same formula as its Western counterparts—two perky hosts sitting in front of a fake fire, with an attractive newsreader on the side. This time Alexander is my translator. We are already assuming the buddy relationship that will emerge in the film. I ad-lib, as much to myself as to our audience of an estimated 100 million people, "Have a great day wherever you are in this huge, wonderful country." So much for eliminating clichés from the script!

Next morning, my guts continue misbehaving, perhaps exacerbated by a growing concern that, since that first busy day, I haven't worked. The scene where Adrian gets killed is still being filmed, so I occupy the time shopping for extra wardrobe with Annie. Fashion-wise, she is everything I'm not—fast and decisive.

We even find a shop that sells American clothes just by the Petrovsky Passazh, an arcade of lavish boutiques touting cashmere and crocodile and $2,000 Yves Saint Laurent shoes that puts Bond Street and Rodeo Drive to shame. Dior, Chanel, Valentino, and Gucci are cheek by elegant jowl in a display of what can only be called "oligar-chic"!

What a Jekyll and Hyde place this is. On the one hand, there are pensioners who describe the last chaotic decade as "like living through a longer and more painful 9/11"; on the other, Russia now accounts for 10 percent of Versace's worldwide sales, and Armani sells more beaded evening gowns in Moscow than in any other world capital. A collective memory of recent socialist penury is apparently what spurs so many newly moneyed Russians to shop and spend.

After much more modest purchases and a quick lunch, Annie and I set off for the *Moscow Heat* press conference that has been scheduled at today's film location in the suburbs. It turns out to be an ugly, abandoned factory, especially uninviting in the continuing drizzle. Despite its distance from the center of town and the allure of the gorgeous Angelina Jolie, who once played my movie daughter and is today in Moscow promoting her new film about Chechen refugees, the place is full of journalists.

Filming is still taking place, so I serve as an hors d'oeuvre for the hungry press corps. Going from one group to the other, I am upbeat and positive, smiling relentlessly for their cameras. "How do you like Russia and working with Russians?" I'm constantly asked—a question that would most fruitfully be answered at the end of my stay. It's rather like journalists back home who constantly request to hear about "something funny that happened on the set." Of course, amusing things occur, but could anyone, if similarly challenged, remember the trivia of weeks before? We seem to be rapidly heading for a situation in which films will only be advertised by their "amusing" outtakes and bloopers.

I notice that I am being continually referred to as an "intellectual" and a "Shakespearean" actor. Austin Powers must have had his Russian entry visa denied! There also seems to be a nearly universal affection for *Cabaret*. I remember being very touched by a compliment from a St. Petersburg journalist. who said that during the Cold War, movies from the West were few, but several of mine, including *Cabaret*, were shown. "They were like old friends," he commented.

Adrian is still being killed, but eventually the shooting of both guns and film stops, and executives and actors gather behind a long table, facing a firing squad of TV cameras and flashbulbs. More young assistants, temporarily liberated from the Czar Pictures office, boost our audience. Banners testifying to our several sponsors enliven the dreary, rain-slicked concrete walls. The conference is protracted—a huge, irritating intrusion into the rapidly shrinking workday.

My mood is not exactly elevated by the news: I will not be working tomorrow either. For the first time, something like panic sets in. This condition is not helped by an inability to communicate elsewhere, as the hotel e-mail is malfunctioning. Perhaps it's all due to the feisty zeitgeist—August has always been a fraught time in Russia. It was the month of the anti-Yeltsin coup, the ruble meltdown, and, more recently, the sinking of the *Kursk* submarine.

Staying in all evening reading to distract myself, I feel a certain kinship with Charles Lamb. "I love to lose myself in other men's minds," he wrote, "when I am not walking, I am reading; I cannot sit still and think. Books think for me." Pat manages to reach me again next morning, and providing further good news, the e-mail is functioning anew and I make up for lost communication time.

At least, I try to. I'm an information age cripple, one of a lost generation of nontyping pen pushers brought up woefully ignorant of this now essential skill.

Resolving to do more constructive things with my day, I arrange to go out to the set and at least get my costumes finally coordinated. While waiting to hear back from the wardrobe department, I indulge in Charles Lamb's other passion, another walk—this time a literary one. In a frame of mind for Nikolay Gogol, after pausing at the base of his brooding statue, I visit the confining rooms where the writer's own pent-up moodiness drove him to hurl the manuscript of *Dead Souls* into the fireplace. Moving on up the Garden Ring, once the social boundary of the city with the plebeians on the outside and the well-to-do within, I arrive at the Chekhov house, now a museum. It was here that the good doctor entertained Tchaikovsky, and wrote *The Seagull* and *The Three Sisters.* Sadly the place is closed for an upgrade, but one day I'll get there, and I'll work, and life will have meaning. . . .

Pressing on to Mikhail Bulgakov country and noticing few dogs in the streets and certainly less of their fouling, I reach the Patriarch's Ponds, a sort of muddy urban lake being noisily renovated. It was here that the devil appeared in that satirical masterpiece, *The Master and Margarita,* which so amusingly lampooned the old system. The midday bells, ringing from St. Simon Stylite church, compel me to enter, and I murmur a quick prayer for the success of our film. A woman there mumbles other imprecations, kissing each icon in turn, but I'm reluctant to go that far. Behind the beautiful church looms a hideous high-rise. "Where God has his church," the locals say, "the devil will have his chapel."

Back at the hotel, there's still no word from the set. "What good is sitting alone in your room?" Indeed. The familiar refrain goads me back outside and over to Kitai Gorod, the oldest part of Moscow, where the narrow streets testify to its being settled since the thirteenth century. Three hundred years later, it formed the core of what was then the world's biggest city. Now full of quaint craft shops, churches, and cathedrals, they seem like doll's houses being set against the vista-mangling backdrop of the monstrous Rossiya Hotel, reputed to be the largest on the planet. One wag claimed it must have been designed by the architect of St. Basil's—but after he had been blinded!

We stayed there in the 1970s, and its functionality outweighed its charm. It was so large that allegedly an enterprising Swiss manager divided it into several distinct hotels. A revisit shows improvements, but its sheer bulk militates against any sense of elegance or intimacy. Wondering if the toilet paper is still like sandpaper and if there are now more than cold cuts on the menu, I sympathize with those fellow visitors who, when the National is overbooked, are sent into exile at the Rossiya. One day, no doubt, when the world has been overrun with minimalist glass box boutique hotels, its solid gilt and concrete architecture is bound to become fashionable and cherished. There's even a strong movement to preserve its older ugly sister, the Moskva Hotel.

The English House is a meticulous reconstruction of the sixteenth-century original, built on this spot as headquarters for the English merchant adventurers who, landing in Russia after failing to find a northern sea route to China, founded the Muscovy Company to trade furs and timber. One had to admire their courage in coming so far. "Moscow is a town I believe to be as large as London," one of their chroniclers, Richard Eden, wrote in 1553, "but very roughly built with no order to it. The roads are exceedingly bad and the people live in the meanest manner. They are wont to drink hard liquors in a quantity amazing to behold." Those early adventurers would hardly recognize the present city, although some habits of the natives would remain reassuringly familiar.

Lined with elaborate treaties and portraits, the museum is guarded by what seem to be a gathering of very friendly old grannies. They point out to me the likeness of Good Queen Bess, who once dabbled with an offer of marriage from Ivan the Terrible. What a dynasty they would have made! I find out too that Spain's Armada was defeated with the help of Russian ropes and timber used in the construction of the English ships. When Peter the Great, unconvincingly disguised as "Peter Mikhailov," was in England learning the shipbuilding trade, he and his retinue were lodged in the house of the poet John Evelyn and succeeded in wrecking the place. "Right nasty" was Evelyn's comment on his rowdy guests. Even his fellow poet John Milton wrote a book about Moscow, and in a strange historical twist on this, Eisenstein's staging of his celebrated battle on the ice in *Alexander Nevsky* was apparently based on Milton's depiction of the war of the angels in *Paradise Lost*.

Later, a phone call reports still further delays with my next scene tomorrow, which will now be a night shoot. A party is announced—also for the morrow. At this, my pent-up frustration boils over. "I didn't come here to party, but to work!" I protest, before slamming down the phone. It is all too reminiscent of a crazy movie I made in 1980 in Montreal—coincidentally standing in for Moscow—in which I played a KGB agent. Cocaine was served as liberally as coffee, and on the third day, I was sternly rebuked for my reluctance to attend a party in honor of the caterers. Given a new script in which my dialogue was left blank, I was informed, in the tones of an adult reproving a naughty child, that I was being paid enough to provide my own.

Bolting outside for a walk under the Kremlin walls, I slowly cool down. There's an air of weekend celebration at odds with my own. The balloons and laughter and innocent pleasures eventually force me to relax, and I resolve to make the best of the situation. After all, why should my standards and practices be imposed on others? As another local saying has it, "Don't go to another's monastery with your own dogma." Film is essentially the result of collaboration, and a party was, after all, just another means of achieving this.

On Sunday, a lurking vestige of the old Puritanism prevails. Refusing to waste a moment, I again give my bodyguard the slip, taking the Metro to visit the Novodevichy Convent and Cemetery. I'm curious to be with normal Muscovites. Deep down, I'm impressed anew with the beauty of the marbled and chandeliered subway stations that also double—God forbid—as air raid shelters. Each of them is differently decorated. One, the futuristic Mayakovskaya, won a prize in the 1938 New York World's Fair, whereas Komsomolskaya displays a mosaic panorama of old Muscovy. The trains come and go with impressive frequency every one and a half minutes. Asked for my autograph—no doubt the result of being so recently on popular television—I notice that many passengers are reading books as well as magazines, testifying to the 98 percent literacy rate achieved in Soviet times.

The Metro station where I get off seethes with humanity, seeming to contradict the current concern that Russia's population is falling by around 700,000 people a year. Apart from losing some 20 million citizens in World War II (revered here as the Great Patriotic War), another cause is that for every ten births, there are thirteen abortions. Easy to obtain in Soviet times, a restraint on them is being put in place. Even so, it is estimated that in ten years the number of children under the age of fifteen will have fallen by a quarter.

Contributing to all this is the effect of environmental poisoning and the huge, grudgingly acknowledged AIDS epidemic.

There is also a high suicide rate that, among young men, is a leading killer. With its manpower stretched and its continent-spanning borders now increasingly difficult to guard, especially in this new age of nuclear terrorism, Russia has a time bomb of a problem. "A creeping catastrophe" is how Putin has described it. A recent *Pravda* report that cosmonauts can conceive children in outer space is no doubt of only little comfort.

It turns out that the reason for the milling multitude is that a football match is about to start at the nearby Luzhniki Stadium, where the 1980 Olympic Games were held. The Novodevichy Convent is a short, unpeopled stroll beyond. Founded in the sixteenth century, it's like a mini-Kremlin, a collection of onion-domed towers set within stout walls overlooking the river. Although Novodevichy means "new maidens," it has nothing to do with novice nuns but refers to the girls who were once sold here into Muslim harems. The place is not exactly a feminist shrine—Peter the Great confined his scheming half sister Sofia here when she threatened his supremacy. From the center of the complex arises the Smolensk Cathedral, and within its pure white walls I discover a service in progress. The singing of the male voice choir, echoing amid the ancient frescos, moves me to tears.

"You are welcome to visit the cemetery," the guidebook insouciantly declares, "where famous Russian and Soviet composers, artists and writers are buried daily except Thursday." Here, adjoining the convent, I find a celebrity culture set in stone, reminiscent of Hollywood's Walk of Fame, but with political stars as well as cultural ones. Nikita Khrushchev and Andrei Gromyko lie alongside Sergei Prokofiev and Dimitri Shostakovich. Prokofiev had the misfortune to die on the same day as Stalin, and the passing of this titan of Russian music went almost unreported. Even in death Stalin controlled the news.

The graves are adorned with huge, elaborate bouquets as well as simple flowers in jam jars. Some monuments have little faded photos appended, as if the live spirit portrayed is trapped within the cold marble and chiseled granite. Khrushchev is shown talking on the phone—the hotline from heaven, I muse, or the other place? Making a pilgrimage along the serried ranks, some long overgrown with trees and weeds, others pristinely polished, I seek out Chekhov and his Olga Knipper and take a Method-like pause in appreciation before the spot marking the great Konstantin Stanislavski's final exit. But I can't find Eisenstein, the legendary film director, and hope that's not another omen!

That evening, impatient to get back to the set, I arrive early. We are filming at a huge nightclub metamorphosed out of an abandoned factory. Called the Casus Conus—Latin, I'm assured, for "falling pins," because the huge complex incorporates several bowling alleys. And that's the least of it. There are also billiard tables, Las Vegas–style gambling, a large restaurant, a cigar room, a pistol range, and the new Russian rage, a sushi bar. This country continues to amaze.

After a quick hair trim, I speak to Jeff, who reassures me that, despite last week's protracted shooting, we should still finish on schedule. Meanwhile, the standard filmmaking mantra, "Hurry up and wait," prevails. While the generator is fired up and the set lit, we are invited by the roundly hospitable club owner, Slava, into his inner sanctum, where sushi is served and his children are introduced. Adrian Paul and Richard Tyson play blackjack with two beautiful lady croupiers. I became slightly allergic to gambling while making a movie in Las Vegas, finding the strange energy of that unnatural, clockless, rhinestoned place to be very depressing. One day, unable to stand it any longer, I rushed out into the street, hailed a passing cab, and asked to be transported to the peace and quiet of the nearby desert. By incredible good fortune I had stopped a driver who habitually went there to meditate, and he was happy to share with me his own favorite, pulse-calming places.

Finally everything is ready, and we film a simple shot of Robert Madrid and myself arriving at the club. It feels good to be in business again—even briefly. My only misgiving is that the establishment is so trendy that there's not a syllable of Cyrillic script in evidence—people might think we did this on the cheap back in LA. Like most of his contemporaries, Jeff watches the action through a monitor. It used to be that directors sat by the camera observing every nuance of the performance and subtly encouraging the actors with their presence. Monitors were originally employed to ensure the integrity of action shots. Now, in our screen-centered age, they are almost universally used to check the entire shoot. But tonight at least, Jeff is justified in using one—he's directing himself in the small but significant role of Alexander's doomed cop sidekick. Moreover, he's playing the scene in Russian, and I admire his energy.

It's raining again as I leave with a nagging backache, perhaps caused by the damp air or some other psychosomatic prompting. But at least we have made a start. Unless there is a major, insuperable problem and production is halted—something not unknown in the perilous world of filmmaking—there is now no going back. The die has been cast in this supreme game of chance.

Четыре · 4

Are My Blinkers Showing?

Moscow does not believe in tears.
— RUSSIAN PROVERB

The *Moscow Times* proclaims the city to be the forty-sixth most expensive in the world, with Oslo improbably taking top honors. Another survey—more accurate, I think—puts it in second place after Hong Kong. I notice that my suite charges a sleep-chasing sum for the night. Fortunately for Muscovites, I read elsewhere that salaries here have tripled since the millennium.

Still falls the rain and, being Monday, the museums are closed, so I spend the morning at the Business Center. I'm now a regular—the girls even know which computer and chair I prefer. Catching up on e-mails, I arrange to fly back to the United States via Washington because I've been asked to perform in a benefit at the Kennedy Center. Special flowers are ordered for my mother's special, biblical four score years and ten birthday.

I enjoy lunch back at the Vogue Café, where the food is not merely fashionable but remarkably good. It has its own nurseries outside the city providing year-round wild strawberries and arugula.

Moscow is now at the stage that Britain was some twenty years ago when, following a long postwar era of indifferent grub, the situation was spectacularly reversed in a culinary revolution. It used to be that every ambitious young man, particularly those from the less fortunate classes whose inelegant vowels were more an asset than a drawback, wanted to be a photographer like the cockney David Bailey, or indeed like myself in *Smashing Time,* shot in authentic "swinging London." Today they all want to be chefs.

Sending some items to the laundry, I notice on the "men's closes" list a garment called "blinkers." It recalls a notice I saw in another eastern European hotel: "The flattening of underwear with pleasure is the job of the chambermaid." Having been three long weeks on the road, I'm getting tired of my unvarying wardrobe but have never been an ardent shopper. Like many actors, I prefer to collect my clothes from movie roles. I have a magnificent camel hair coat that was tailor-made for my role in the sumptuously stylish *Murder on the Orient Express.* Decades later, I was reunited with it on another film and, seizing this unlikely chance, purchased it: we are now inseparable. Some of my best things came from the young Gianni Versace when he was also designing clothes for the movies. I also have my sleek, black "Sandman" outfit from *Logan's Run,* but that nylon fashion no-no has stayed firmly in the closet for three decades!

There's good and bad news. The call sheet arrives with a shot list, which suggests a welcome new degree of preparedness. There's also a note from the hotel requesting me to discontinue the use of my little traveling kettle to make early morning tea when confrontation with a waiter is least welcome. How can they deny me this innocent pleasure, especially in the year marking the centenary of that quintessence of civilization, the teabag? My kettle has served me faithfully all over the world and especially in areas with water of dubious quality. Apparently it's a fire hazard—but surely not as dangerous as Lytton Strachey's Indian servant, for example, who used to cook chapattis on the living room carpet. I should now order a samovar for the room, which at least would be in perfect harmony with the decor.

Discovering that the maids are still spying on the clientele is a little disconcerting. It must be the one who daily rearranges my toilet articles, lining them up like soldiers in a Red Square parade. Surely a Young Pioneer in the old days, she's perhaps the one responsible for "flattening the underwear," military style.

Everything seems back-to-front the next day when my dawn call catches Pat just as she's going to bed. My driver sets off for the nightclub in early morning daylight and then blithely charges the wrong way up a one-way street. Unadorned with neon, the Casus Conus looks desolate and forlorn in its nondescript setting beset with drizzle—like someone wearing evening clothes on the morning bus.

It's getting cold. The news is chilly too: the international discussions over North Korea's nuclear program make our film seem alarmingly relevant. Katrina, an American student working with us as an assistant, confirms that this is one of the wettest, coldest summers on record. Jeff, though, is perversely delighted—he wants that shiny, wet street look. *Cool Moscow,* I suggest, would be a more appropriate title for our film—and certainly less of an overt homage to Schwarzenegger's *Red Heat.* But at least no one is dying of the temperature here.

Much of the morning is spent filming Nikolay's cronies, the cigar-chomping, vodka-swilling gang bosses who are assembled with their molls. The closest I ever came to the real thing was an encounter in Sochi with a flamboyant individual who flaunted his wealth with a collection of fabulous villas, icons, Japanese armor, and luxury cars. He only wanted to get into the movie business so that his daughters could gain kudos at their elite English boarding school.

Richard Tyson's hair has been dyed bright blond. Now he is as arresting as our prop master Yuri, who favors colored punk haircuts that look as if they were styled with a lawnmower. I think ruefully of past cinematic dye jobs of my own—the raven black Capulet coiffure, for example, or the blond mop of curls acquired to play Marty Feldman's improbable twin brother. We shoot a scene with the handheld steadycam that smoothly follows Robert and me up the metal staircase, as go-go girls gyrate and smoke diffuses the garish lighting. Our diurnal nightclubbers seem unfailingly cheerful and patient, but extra extras are needed to enlarge the crowd. Our usually casually clad assistants are coopted and astonish by appearing in chic dresses and suave suits. Even John Aronson wields his light meter wearing a tuxedo.

We continue the scene the next day. Between takes, Tony and his assistant Philip teach me some warm-up exercises, and I wonder what physical extravagances they have in mind for the big duel. My much-eluded bodyguard is now stationed on the set; apparently Adrian has been bothered by a persistent drunk, but the only minor intrusion on my time comes from extras requesting autographs and photographs.

They remind me of my own first movie job—as an extra—while I was a student at Oxford. Dirk Bogarde had come to town to make *The Mind Benders*, and many of the university acting fraternity volunteered to animate the background. One kept a respectful distance from the stars, despite longing to talk to them about their work. It was serendipitous that, only a few years later, I should find myself back at Oxford filming in Joseph Losey's *Accident*—again as a student, even wearing the same clothes, and again with Dirk

Bogarde. But this time I was a fellow film actor, greedily devouring all he had to say about my brand-new profession.

At least our extras are polite, unlike the woman who, just before we left for Russia, forced her way into our house, asking me to pose with her bewildered child. My bodyguard would have been useful then. Now he solemnly escorts me the ludicrously short distance to and from my trailer. Even the hotel seems to be getting in on the protection racket: I get messages marked "Michael Incognito York."

At lunch the caterer chastises me for not eating more, and I compliment her—most sincerely—on the hot and nourishing food that she brings in daily to each location. The film army definitely marches on its stomach. I once worked on an Italian production that, after shooting in Rome, moved to North Africa with a huge convoy of vehicles. Pride of place was given to the truck carrying the pasta. A British crew is incapable of functioning without regular visits from the tea trolley, while their American colleagues are spoiled with a daylong feast of goodies.

Much of the afternoon is spent setting up a shot where our Russian stuntmen fall to the ground from an upper balcony. Looking alarmingly tough, they reputedly used live ammunition on the other set. However, despite deploying impressive ropes, counterweights, harnesses, and mattresses, all their lengthy preparation ends in a miscalculation with one of them falling on his head. He seems none the worse for it, but our tight schedule has been knocked on its head too. My first meeting with Alexander—an important moment because it introduces two lead characters—is rushed into one quick, all-encompassing shot. Alexander informs me that our TV appearance had huge ratings and they want us back. Yes, but will we have a completed film to talk about?

A dawn wake-up call intended for another room rouses me reluctantly. On the early TV news there are reports of a shooting in

Chicago, replete with SWAT teams, ambulances, and victims—
the U.S. equivalent of the scene we filmed last night. But at least
the weatherman promises brighter, fairer weather. Hooray.

I have coffee with Mila, a friend who divides her time between
Russia and the United States, where she has businesses. It must be
a shock for her that office rents in Moscow are now the third highest in Europe. We chat about other changes that have occurred
since we first met at Pat's exhibition in St. Petersburg a few years
ago. President Putin, it seems, is fostering renewed national pride.
Recognizing a lingering nostalgia for the Soviet Union, he has
even restored the old national anthem—but with some discreet
word changes. May Day, the former Day of Workers Solidarity,
has been similarly retained as a national holiday but softened into
the less aggressive Day of Spring and Labor.

Certainly the old KGB has returned as an influence; its former
officers, including the president, now fill major political offices.
Despite the media being slowly reined in and the gradual loss of
checks and balances, there is a feeling that Putin should be given
a chance. At least he is a welcome change from the ailing geron-
tocracy that ruled a moribund Soviet Union.

Mila tells me that she too is feeling the cold and even wears a fur
coat. Her thoughtful parting gift to me, in case I should ever have
need of it, is *der-mo,* the Russian for "bullshit"! There's a biting
wind lashing the street outside when I'm picked up for work. We're
back at Tsaritsino, and back in America, to complete the close-ups
of the scene left unfinished on that first, fraught morning and to
pick up a shot of Robert and myself with the mourners outside the
now deserted church. The hairspray can is in constant hissing use
as the gusts, as unruly as my coiffure, whip across the scene.

It's a relief to move inside one of the gloomy palaces, although
the long abandoned building is dangerously underlit, cold as a
tomb, and suffused with centuries of dust. Thanks to Natasha's

foresight, I'm wearing a warm turtleneck sweater as well as a suede jacket. A scene between Alexander and me, after we have been captured and chained up by Nikolay, is played simply and goes well. I'm pleased as it's a crucial one, with more useful back story where we both probe beneath each other's defenses, initiating the unlikely process of bonding. By the time we finish at one o'clock in the morning, the temperature has plunged to 9 degrees Fahrenheit. Now I begin to understand why Napoleon lost and why those pioneer Englishmen bartered so furiously for furs!

Good day, sunshine! The upbeat weather guy delivers on his promise next morning when more cast members, Joanna Pacula and Andrew Divoff, arrive. I take Joanna for the ritual walk around the cordons of a sunlit Red Square, returning by way of the GUM store. She is as astonished as Pat and I were by the transformation. The wind has dropped, but people are still wearing warm clothes. Sure enough, after the morning's brief luminous, teasing outburst, the sullen clouds whirl back in again.

Traveling slowly back to Tsaritsino through clogged streets, the driver makes his usual U-turn in order to head in the right direction. Strictly schooled in LA traffic, I'm curious to see if the police will one day pull him over for this transgression. The limo has been stopped once, but only because the cop was my driver's friend. Perhaps they will pick on me instead: Moscow's finest are notorious for hitting on foreigners and issuing instant fines.

While Alexander is being roughed up on the set by Nikolay's thugs, I go for a walk in the woods. It feels good to get outside again, but my sylvan rapture is curtailed when I come across Tony rehearsing the basics of my upcoming saber duel alfresco. How are we going to film it safely in so short a time?

I think enviously of the long training period for the duels on Franco Zeffirelli's *Romeo and Juliet,* where the fights were so meticulously rehearsed that we could have done them in our sleep. And just as well too. In a stroke of genius, Zeffirelli changed the location of Tybalt's duel with Romeo from a flat, level space to a steeply graveled slope, giving the sword and dagger skirmish a dangerous, off-kilter momentum. "He jests at scars that never felt a wound." I was somewhat bemused to later learn from Zeffirelli that I was complimented for playing the role "in the Russian style" when the film premiered in the Soviet Union. I'm still unclear what that is.

There is further pressure to finish Richard Tyson's work so that he can move on to another job. To speed things along, Whitney tells me, we may use one of Tsaritsino's buildings for the interior of the government office and even convert the lake into the Moscow River waterfront. Such instant adaptability is the hallmark of independent filmmaking.

Toward evening, the ghostly white limo materializes to convey me home. My requests for a more modest vehicle have come to nothing, and I give in gracefully. I know the producers are only trying to please me, and I don't want to upset them. Perhaps it's a Russian standard: Alexander tells me that he is always chauffeured in Moscow.

I'm reminded of a similar situation in Zagreb in 1994 during the Balkan war. There to make a film, *Gospa,* with Martin Sheen, Pat and I were picked up on arrival at the deserted airport by a huge, white stretch limo. Protesting that such a vehicle was perhaps inappropriate at such a time—especially with its sitting-duck visibility as a target—we were told that the producers wanted us to have the kind of vehicle we were accustomed to in Los Angeles. It seemed ungracious to mention that neither of us would ever dream of hiring such overblown transportation, so we kept quiet, enduring the behemoth's laborious sixteen-point turns as it negotiated narrow village streets. On the other hand, Dominique Lapierre, Pat's first Moscow guide and the ebullient author of so many equally revelatory books, told us that such a conveyance proved remarkably effective when he first went to India to research his book *Freedom at Midnight.* He drove there in an antique Rolls-Royce, the crowds parting reverently before him as if greeting the return of some long-awaited maharajah.

We speed home alongside the Moscow River, attracting no undue attention from the natives. Almost every building is floodlit, and the effect is superb. Watch out Paris—your City of Light title is being challenged!

My mother is ninety years old today, August 30. I call her at home in Sussex, England. She has been unwell and has weakened since I visited her a few weeks ago en route to Russia. She tells me that this was the last occasion that she ventured out of her meticulously maintained house. I give her a brief review of life in Moscow, but even talking is an effort for her now.

I remember nostalgically the time in the mid-1960s, when I was making my first film in Rome, and my mother came to stay in the little apartment I had rented. I was happy to be able to share with her some of the dolce vita that I was then experiencing. My parents have always supported my acting ventures but without being demanding or intrusive. I only recently discovered a scrapbook recording my career that my father had kept. Unlike Alexander's mother, moreover, he withheld the bad reviews.

Breakfasting with Joanna, I happen to mention that our hotel has use of a golf course, whereupon she reveals that she is a passionate golfer who, when not acting, delights in the sport, playing the charity circuit. Immediately booking a round, she spends the rest of the meal waxing lyrical over such mysteries as graphite drivers and birdies. Golf, once dismissed as a bourgeois novelty, has only recently been taken up here. Like tennis, it is gaining ground, and there is even a Russian Open championship. Playing in the snow must be a unique handicap.

While Joanna heads off for the links, I make a pilgrimage to the Stanislavski House Museum but discover it is open only in the afternoon. It recently lost a great part of its invaluable collection in a disastrous fire, and I fear for objects seen on display elsewhere that seem to lack adequate protection. Instead, I head for 17 Ulitsa Nikolskaya, where the Slavyansky Bazaar hotel used to stand.

It was here in 1898 that Stanislavski and the playwright and fellow director Vladimir Nemirovich-Danchenko had their fateful meeting. Over an all-day lunch, they formulated plans to found the Moscow Art Theater and reform contemporary drama to be more realistic and respect the writer's intentions. As Stanislavski wrote, "We declared war on all the conventionalities of the theatre—in the acting, the properties, the scenery, and the interpretation of the play."

Because the Russian language has no definite or indefinite articles, Stanislavski's teachings, offered as "a method" for acting, have been monumentalized in the misunderstanding West into "The Method." Above all, Stanislavski was a pragmatist, even changing his mind about the supremacy of emotional recall over physical detail in the actor's bag of tricks, a development little heeded by such inflexible gurus as Lee Strasberg.

The brides are out posing again—it must be Saturday—as we return to the set through gray streets. Pat calls en route, and I give her a virtual tour, pointing out the newly familiar landmarks like a chatty guide. Nazar is discovered asleep in my trailer, obviously having spent the night there. I admire his fortitude. Our relationship is now much more relaxed. He's stopped being the overattentive, immaculate Jeeves and has metamorphosed into a sort of assistant, indistinguishable from the others. Even the china plates have been replaced with plastic.

For the most part, Nazar leaves me alone, but today, slumped in the driver's seat behind a curtain partition, he's watching a small portable TV whose tinny insistence grates on my nerves. But, feeling sorry for his impossibly long working hours—I learned that filming went on till three this morning—I wait before asking him to switch it off. Chunks of cheese and meat snacks add pungency to the shared air.

Besides working on the script, I enjoy jotting down observations. I have always found the abstract, isolated nature of movie trailers to be highly conducive to literary consumption and output. And I'm not alone in this. When filming *The Last Remake of Beau Geste* with Peter Ustinov in Spain, I was impressed to see him emerge from his trailer each day with fresh chapters for his memoirs.

I take a stroll through the leafy gloom of the park, sodden confetti underfoot. The ruined buildings stand stark against the skyline like the setting of some eighteenth-century gothic horror novel. When I return, my *The Three Musketeers* is romping energetically along on Nazar's little TV set, and we watch the scene of the fight on the frozen pond. It was filmed in the middle of a blazingly hot Spanish summer on "ice" created out of slippery paraffin wax and huge chunks of polystyrene. Give or take the extremes in the weather, nothing much has changed over the decades—here I am about to duel on another set inhospitable to normal human activity!

Sunday brings a saddening e-mail about my mother from my doctor brother-in-law, Mark: "We visited May for her 90th Birthday. Although frail, she enjoyed her lunch. It's impossible to give a time scale—realistically, it is probably a matter of weeks rather than months. Will keep you posted." At least I feel relatively close at hand here in Europe, should her health suddenly worsen.

Driving back to the set with Richard Tyson, we reminisce about locations we have shared, particularly Morocco, where I have happily filmed several times and Richard worked on *Black Hawk*

Down. He also spent many grueling months filming as Genghis Khan in Mongolia, only to have the results of all that work imprisoned in an Italian bank vault, pending the resolution of a financial dispute. Given our producers' enthusiasm and determination, I'm confident this won't happen with our present venture, but filming is one of those risky businesses in which nothing is guaranteed.

Discovering that Richard is also a golf enthusiast, I introduce him to Joanna, and they delightedly plot a game on their next day off. Today we are filming the special forces raid, so the set is bristling with military hardware and personnel. Thirty of Moscow's finest SWAT forces, along with forty spit-and-polished militia, have been hired to give the scene an alarming authenticity. There are soldiers in balaclavas and military fatigues, Kalashnikovs, and even a tank. Images of the recent SWAT team raid on Moscow's Dubrovka Theater flash uncomfortably to mind.

It's Joanna's first day of filming, and she looks very fetching in a black combat suit and cap. Sasha Izotov is playing the chief of police, appearing equally elegant in uniform. His producer's hat exchanged for a military one as large as a halo, he's holding a pipe—a good idea, as actors never know what to do with their hands. Our little scene together goes well. We play it more seriously than written, reasoning that, at this point in the story, it's warranted by the situation, there having been enough death and mayhem. We have that last farewell scene at the airport for some appropriate banter.

"Not bad for a couple of civilians," is Sasha's parting line, to which I respond, in reference to the day's considerable production values, "Not bad for a couple of new producers!"

After lunch, the tank crew invites me inside the horribly cramped and claustrophobic vehicle, letting me operate the periscope and the gun—the closest I ever want to get to the reality of war. There are numerous heartfelt vodka toasts to peace and co-operation and smiling group photos. The rain holds off, although a dramatically scudding sky races over the inner courtyard like a speeded-up movie. The scene being filmed is the auction of the nuclear suitcase, presumably one of the eighty that have gone missing since Soviet times—a key plot detail that makes our story alarmingly contemporary.

But today the crooks are sent packing. Soldiers rappel down the inside walls to round them up while a helicopter hovers noisily overhead. Then we film the climax of my duel with Nikolay, like the shoot-out between the sheriff and the bad guy in an old western. After I run him through with a sword, Richard does a hair-raisingly realistic and, as far as I can judge, unprotected death fall down a flight of steps.

By far the most dramatic scene is being enacted offstage. One of our American crew has been having a rather indiscreet affair with a Russian assistant, whose enraged husband has come to the set with a gun, seeking vengeance. The poor misguided man could not have chosen a worse time or place in which to wield a weapon. He is spotted by one of the hired professionals, who threatens to shoot him unless he desists from his rampage.

At dusk I scan the horizon for Mars, which is now reputed to be as close to the earth as it was in Neanderthal times. But today's polluted skies prevent me from seeing it. Maybe it's the close proximity of this contentious planet that, as so often in Shakespeare's plays, is causing all the production problems! Later that evening, back inside the dust bowl, we set up the scene where I'm menaced by Nikolay's girlfriend, Mascha, played by the svelte Maria Golubkina, reworking it to be a little less *Grand Guignol*.

Again there are delays—this time while Maria is made up, even though she has long been waiting in her trailer. A few days ago it was because she was away doing a TV interview. "Nothing must be done hastily but the killing of fleas" goes a local saying, and its peasant philosophy seems pervasive. The wrong priorities seem still to prevail. Although we have six wardrobe assistants, there is no real script supervisor—arguably the most important job on the set that three different people have already attempted to master.

Another reason for the slowness is that the camera has only one magazine that has to be laboriously removed and the film changed while all activity is suspended. Whitney reckons that this is cumulatively costing us about two hours a day. When it was suggested that two or more magazines, as is customary elsewhere, would enable the filming to proceed more quickly and efficiently, especially in the middle of a shot, it was refused as not being the Russian way of doing things. Camera crews here seem to have different duties to their western counterparts. The sweet, shy man who performs the tediously repetitive task of changing magazines is weighed down by a comically huge mustache and glasses with lenses as thick as bottle bottoms. But apparently they function well because the developed film is invariably in focus.

I discover that Maria speaks French, and we chat about local working habits. "Why all these avoidable delays?" I ask. "Surely the crew would also like to go home earlier." "It's in our spirit," she replies with a mixture of resignation and pride, even though Maria is the epitome of the new breed—pencil slim and married to a racing driver. It all seems like a holdover from Soviet times when workers insisted that "as long as they pretend to pay us, we will pretend to work."

Things are incomparably worse in Armenia, according to Hiner Saleem, an Iraqi Kurd director who has just been filming there. Interviewed by the *International Herald Tribune,* he states that "When you are told 'problem nyet,' it means that there will be a lot of problems ahead. When you are told 'just a minute,' it means two or three days. When you're told 'tomorrow,' it means never." At least our results so far seem promising. Gib Jaffe, our editor, is also working here in Moscow and is enthusiastic. His is another crucial job on the movie. It's no coincidence that many distinguished filmmakers started their careers by learning how to piece together and pace film.

Finally everything is ready. Maria, poured provocatively into a shiny black dress à la femme Nikita, straddles my lap as I'm lashed to a chair, menacing me with a sharp knife and her seductive presence. We film until one in the morning. The pressure to finish has an elegant payoff—instead of an elaborate and improbable fight with her, Alexander dispatches Maria with a simple twist of her head in his massive hands.

Пять · 5

Location, Location, Location

Without stooping down for the mushroom,
you cannot put it in your basket.
— RUSSIAN PROVERB

I t's the first day of September—Labor Day in the United States
and summer's unofficial end. Perversely, summer has made a
belated reappearance with clear blue skies that encourage another
city walk.

Heading for a neighborhood to the northeast of the National
called Zemlyanoi Gorod, distinguished by its numerous classical
mansions and literary associations, I am well rewarded. It's an
area honeycombed with old streets, full of elegant homes and
quiet gardens that reflect the original builder's eclectic and varie-
gated tastes. This charming confectionary of pastel stucco and art
deco basks in its memories in the warm sun. One imposing
building, with deco frescos portraying antique Greek and Russian
literary gods, was a brothel for the intelligentsia. The old-world
ambiance is enhanced by the presence of numerous little girls
wearing elaborate hair bows and old-fashioned uniforms, heading

back to class for the first day of the new school year. September 1 is a special day on the Russian school calendar.

Passing Cooks Street, with its adjoining roads all named after culinary paraphernalia, I detour to the Arbat. This was once the most beloved street in Moscow, the artistic heart of the nineteenth-century city. Now, like the once fashionable Carnaby Street in London, it is the tired refuge of souvenir shops and cheap cafés. This is where Pushkin lived with his beloved Natalia—their home is now a museum—and despite its present decrepitude, the street still haunts the collective memory in contemporary song.

Back at the hotel, I grab a quick lunch with Richard Tyson, who is paying for his spectacular death fall with some spectacular bruises. After my recent physical activity, everything aches inordinately, and before the evening rush begins, I head for the pool with its invigorating jacuzzi and calming fish tank. That night, our producers inveigle us into another party back at the nightclub location. I accept. It's been a tough week, and this time we've earned it. Joanna declines as she is filming tomorrow, and I feel that my earlier punctilious (or, as I prefer, professional) stand has been somewhat validated.

But the party turns out to be essentially another press conference with hordes of waiting journalists, cameras, and recorders at the ready. It's now late, since rain held up transportation, and I don't have the energy to deal with this before at least eating something. So, running their gauntlet, I head upstairs where other exhausted crew members, who could have been enjoying a day off, have been corralled. Even our megahero Alexander confesses to being tired and I order his beautiful wife, Katya, to take him home—to no avail, of course. The food, though, is Lucullan and I wolf down caviar and blinis in between posing for cameras and answering questions from the press who have found their way upstairs.

Having now done something in the movie possibly worth talking about, I live up to the letter of my contract. A journalist tells me that Val Kilmer failed to show up for his press conference and, as much as I almost sympathize with him, I'm glad I accepted this invitation. There are speeches and toasts and leading cast members are presented with large, beautifully crafted picnic hampers. For some inexplicable reason, I am singled out to be also given a white-bearded garden gnome, with which I abscond into the wet night about midnight.

There's nothing but bad news in the morning paper. And it's still raining. Richard and I struggle back to Tsaritsino through unusually choked streets. Our set looks even more somber and uninviting in the gray gloom; Catherine the Great must have seen it on just such a day when she ordered it to be pulled down. I place my gnome, now named Tolstoy, by the trailer door, hoping he will bring me good luck for the climactic fight with Richard to be filmed today. "Tea?" Nazar enquires—this greeting now takes precedence over "good morning."

Richard and I first work out a sequence with Tony, rehearse it, and then film it—and then go on to the next. Although not ideal, this is a relatively safe procedure. I've suffered too many injuries when overtaxed memory is allied to imprecise directions and physical tiredness. My rubber-soled shoes are more than proving their worth.

We cut and thrust away all day long in the insalubrious, vaulted chamber, obediently trying to live up to that repeatedly exhorted word, "Action!" To keep alert, I imagine I can hear Katchachurian's lively "Sabre Dance" pulsating in the background. Bolstering Tolstoy's gnomic presence, I visualize myself surrounded by a protective cocoon of white light. I'll try anything, especially after discovering that the stuntman in the nightclub fall broke his leg.

Somewhat set in their ways, the Russian stunt performers have resisted Tony's more choreographic demands.

I'm discovering the *Moscow Heat* diet—not much real food
after 5:00 P.M. apart from Snickers bars. One of the assistants
found out that I'm partial to these energy-boosting marvels and
left a small horde of them in my trailer. They are far too easy to
find in Moscow—my nearest fix is in the underground pedestrian crossing by the hotel, just by the bootlegged tapes and the
ladies selling plastic jewelry that glows in the dark. Somewhere
around one o'clock of a damp, chilly morning, Richard and I are
both exhausted—and fearful of any resulting mishap. Not even
Alexander's hated steroids would have had any effect at this
point. Fortunately Richard has agreed to stay on a few days over
his scheduled stop date, so we can complete the fight with a second unit under Tony's still relentlessly enthusiastic direction.

Some vandal smashed little Tolstoy to pieces. I'm fed up with
this location—it's distant, dirty, and dangerous. How, I wonder,
can our profession ever be thought of as glamorous? The curtains
in my trailer have artificial butterflies pinned to them, and I'm
beginning to feel like one of them. They remind me of a production of Chekhov's *Three Sisters* where a key feature of the décor
was a framed picture containing three mounted butterflies, forever pinned down.

The schizoid sun deigns to return the next day, flooding into
the breakfast room. This meal has become an unthinking, unvarying routine: fruit, blinis, eggs, black bread, and the *Moscow
Times*. I even feel affronted if I don't get my usual window seat.
Afterward, still aching all over, especially where whacked and
whirled into the wall, I decide on another soak in the jacuzzi till
pickup time at 1:00 P.M., despite the alluring beauty of the day
and my own restless curiosity to see more.

September 3 is my parents' sixty-fourth wedding anniversary. I have photographs of them taken on that day—so young and happy, even though my father was to leave the next day to fight in a war that eventually took him to Berlin and into contact with the Russian forces. I recall his red sector armband, emblazoned with our ally's hammer and sickle, that he gave me to play with as a child.

Andrew Divoff joins me on the drive to the Kiev railway station, where we will be playing a scene together, he as a traitorous U.S. embassy official who turns up the Moscow heat. A recent dinner with an aunt who lives here, he tells me, was considerably enlivened by the presence of her two pet crows. Among the least of his depredations, Ivan the Terrible reputedly expelled the crows from Moscow. However, demonstrating that every tyrant's sway is limited, the birds are back. But not the sunshine. Exhausted by its early efforts, this too northernly sun has again given up, returning the city to its now customary cool grayness.

There's a lively crowd outside the station, milling around its many slot machines, kiosks, and bars and hauling bulky wheeled bags. It has the honky-tonk atmosphere common to these busy places. Like most of the terminals constructed during the golden age of train travel, it has a huge arched canopy of glass and steel spanning its interior. I have an instant flash of déjà vu. Three decades ago during the making of *Cabaret* in Lübeck, Germany, its *Hauptbahnhof* was standing in for Berlin's. I had the time-warped pleasure of seeing myself arrive there young and inexperienced and, in the very next take, leave full of the extraordinary experiences imprinted by those fervent times.

I half expect to see Anna Karenina come sweeping down the platform amid the whistles and smoke of her fateful steam engine. Now trains with uniformed stewardesses and lace-curtained windows are hauled off by giant electric engines to such romantic-sounding destinations as Lvov and Odessa. A nonstop loudspeaker intones information. There is a news report of a bomb on a train in the southern Stavropol region, reminding us of the dangers lurking even here. However, it feels good to be out of our dusty hellhole and inside this spacious glass cathedral.

Our film unit crowds the platform among the milling passengers. Someone's sitting in my name-emblazoned chair, but I have to sympathize—everyone is getting weary and there are never enough seats. As has been said of playing Shakespeare, "It's so tiring—nobody gets to sit down unless you're a king." The accumulation of so many long days' journeys into night has shortened tempers. Jeff is supremely frustrated that his unit production manager has already sent back needed equipment. Even the scene to be filmed is about betrayal; I'm double-crossed by my supposed friend in the U.S. embassy. I get annoyed when shown the tabloid photos taken at the nightclub. Naturally I am portrayed openmouthed, guzzling blinis. When I phone Pat, I find her anxious too, about having her prints ready on time.

Once the sequence is completed, I lie down in my trailer as Nazar drives it to the next location and enjoy a passing cityscape of rooftops, spires, and lights. We set up in a luxurious restaurant so new and spotless that it looks like a set. Having to use a cell phone in the next scene, I come up against a salient feature of this production—product placement. The film has numerous private corporate sponsors who expect a publicity return on their investment. So the cell phone is conspicuously displayed, as is the Parliament vodka bottle on the table. It has now starred in more scenes than a good many of the cast.

Acting while tired produces a relaxed, unfussy performance, and my scene with Joanna and Alexander goes well. When it concludes at two in the morning, Joanna heads directly for an early flight to Poland and a holiday with her family—and no doubt with those graphite drivers too.

The mono life endures—same breakfast, same e-mail routine, same pouring rain. My bones ache and a drowsy numbness pains my senses. Outside the same long, wet, patient lines visit Lenin's tomb. The last and only time we queued to inspect Lenin's waxy remains in 1973 we found ourselves alongside the novelist Penelope Mortimer, the recorder of at least as many unhappy relationships as Chekhov. She remarked how ironic it was for a regime that discouraged the cult of personality to countenance such unbridled idolatry.

Rain is forecast for the next three days. In retrospect my week with Pat seems like a Bergmanesque summer idyll. In New York too, it has been lobbing down liquid for five days on the U.S. Open tennis tournament; as if not to be outdone, the newspaper weather map portrays our region as "unusually cold." Other news is equally grim: the train bomb injured dozens, mostly students, and Russia is considering sending forces to Iraq. Having had oil dealings with Saddam's regime, Russia wants to join in the postwar rush for contracts.

Today we are filming in front of one of Moscow's Seven Sisters—distinctive, ornate ziggurats erected by Stalin to rival the panache of the thrusting American skyline. His architect had worked on highrises there, an experience that providentially saved him from a one-way trip to prison. The rebel poet Yevgeny Yevtushenko lived in one of them in the late 1960s, as did other prominent artists such as the Bolshoi ballerina Galina Ulanova. Yevtushenko wrote feelingly of the price to be paid for such favoritism in his poem "The Cockroaches," alluding to the pestilential KGB spies that infested the building. The "Sisters" are becoming newly fashionable and busy with expensive renovation. But now, outside this one, it is so dark in its hulking shadow that I wonder if any light can penetrate the camera. The persistent rain is not a problem—unless backlit it will not show up on film and provide continuity problems. Even so, John Aronson's usual Buddha-like calm is compromised by a certain irritation.

That evening, to compound the gloom, the Carpetbagger (from the Vogue Café?) calls again. This time he boasts of setting up two films here: I am sphinx-like in my response. Such hype is matched in an amusing film on TV called *Spinning Boris,* showing how three American political consultants used proven U.S. media manipulation techniques to return Yeltsin to office in the Russian election of 1996. Pat and I were in Russia at the time, and I recall seeing the campaign posters lavished around the city, with Boris beaming beefily away like a film star, and had no inkling that this advertising came from Madison Avenue rather than the Kremlin.

In the TV movie, Toronto stands in for Moscow, with footage of the real city intercut. It is so effective that I am glad we are filming at a quintessentially Russian place today, and even more determined to get us out into the streets more often. The newspaper announces that Mikhail Khodorkovsky, the most pro-American oligarch, has purchased the *Moscow News,* hiring a major critic of the present regime to run it. Will there now be a negatively *Spinning Putin*?

My driver is already gray with fatigue when he picks up Richard and me the next day for another early morning commute to Tsaritsino and the conclusion of our fight. Again, he's only managed a few hours' sleep—I hope he'll use the backseat of the limo to catch up. On arrival, nothing seems to be happening. Apparently the weapons we require won't arrive until midday, as the Mosfilm warehouse doesn't open till 11:00. Here we go again—now I understand why it's not unusual for Mosfilm to take a year to make a movie. When the guns eventually arrive they are the wrong ones, nor are the foils needed for the scene with them. These misunder-standings are now referred to as "road to airport" moments. My new hyper-Zen attitude accepts that this is how it is. At least it's not raining.

Richard and I have been condemned to film with the second unit back in the ancient, sneeze-inducing dust. We should be get-ting stunt performers' checks for breathing this filthy air, and indeed many of the more sensible crew members are wearing sur-gical masks. Even before we start I'm hurting all over, especially my blade-wielding wrist. So I arm myself anew with white light, reminding myself that it's only a movie and that I would prefer not to emulate Pushkin by dying needlessly in a duel.

Actually I've been in worse locations. Early in my career in *Accident,* I was trapped upside down in a wrecked car while the leading lady walked over my face. Later, gummed up with fake fur, I was lashed down to Burt Lancaster's grim operating table in *The Island of Dr. Moreau.* One Brazilian director filled every scene—even sunny exteriors—with thick smoke to diffuse the light. Perhaps worst of all was the bloody slaughterhouse in Span-dau, Berlin, that, hung with dripping carcasses, served as the set-ting for a particularly gruesome staged killing. I can handle this . . .

I notice that Richard has a bloody cut and admire his authen-tic makeup. It turns out to be the real thing—a mishap with my double. There must be a masochistic streak in actors' personali-ties that they accept so much physical abuse.

Tony speaks to his assistants, Philip and Lina, in voluble Can-tonese. After the slow, lugubrious Russian vowels, they seem to be screaming insults at each other. But it certainly charges up the at-mosphere. Only nineteen years old, Lina has made herself as in-valuable as Katrina and the other Czarist handmaidens. Speaking

Cantonese, as well as fluent Mandarin, Russian, and English, she is the indispensable link between Tony and the Russian stuntmen. Working all hours and probably for pitiful remuneration, the girls are true heroines, possessing both a sense of humor and that priceless commodity, seemingly so rare in Russia, initiative.

We go to it again and, in between camera setups, Richard and I challenge each other to another duel of Shakespearean speeches that sound wonderful in the empty, echoing space. "This will last out a night in Russia / When nights are longest there," I ruefully recall the Bard writing somewhere. But the Muse of Fire keeps us alert. With every successfully filmed sequence Richard sees "that consummation devoutly to be wished," his safe departure, draw ever closer.

One of the many palace pigeons flutters out of the dark through the lit set, reminding me of another literary image, the Anglo-Saxon concept of life as a bird that flies from the dark storm into the warm, bright hall only to fly out again. Rather like a film—a fleeting spotlit lifetime, intense and dramatic while lived, but eventually over.

Next Sunday is City Day, a big holiday celebrating Moscow's 856th birthday (it was first mentioned in writing in 1147) and one of Mayor Luzhkov's pet projects. We have all been given the day off, not because of the occasion but because traffic is expected to be impassable. Almost every square will be transformed into a stage for every kind of entertainment. As I am driven home, I take in the lights for the coming celebrations twinkling on bridges and buildings, with the whole glittering cityscape reflected in the shining river. Streets have already been blocked, diverting us around even more rings than usual. Finally recognizing a familiar monument in the distance, I ask to be let out to walk home. "Nyet, Gollywood star not valk." We continue to circle, ending up a frustrating half hour later in front of the lit-up National.

A thin, watery morning sun filters through the gray haze, lending an extra brio to the flags flapping bravely in the breeze. Military planes seeded the clouds to guarantee fine weather—and it seems to have worked. Even so, behind my double-glazing, I note that people are warmly dressed. Police are starting to line up at intervals along the silent, traffic-banned street outside.

Pat calls me during breakfast. She's already in bed after canceling dinner plans to concentrate on the crucial final week of preparation. The show will be hung on Monday. This is probably our longest separation in almost thirty-six years of marriage. I've been reading a script about Dylan Thomas, and a beautiful passage from a letter to his Caitlin comes poignantly to mind: "How did I know three months from you could be like the distance from the sun to the earth—only infinitely lonelier."

The street is soon *en fête*—with banners, balloons, and even circus girls in ponytails who parade around on horseback. The relative traffic-free calm gives a suggestion of what the city must have been like as portrayed in old etchings and lithographs, before gas-guzzling, fume-belching monsters invaded the scene, transforming its dynamics forever. A swarthy, leather-jacketed stranger accosts me, and I grab on to my wallet. But he turns out to be my replacement driver. It's lucky he found me in the milling throng, and little short of miraculous that he discovered a parking place nearby.

He makes up for lost time by trying to race round the ring roads that are reputedly wide enough for aircraft to land on. But not today—as predicted, they are clogged with holiday traffic. Once we reach the outer suburbs, however, my Cadillac cosmonaut blasts off, honking and cursing red stop signs, one hand on the wheel, the other on a cell phone yelling to his girlfriend.

The city now streaking by eventually peters out into an alphaville of concrete high-rises set among bare fields and the occasional ancient wooden house, and we pull into a police station—our home away from home for the day. There are delays here too, apparently because the police chief has been promised a fax machine as part of the deal to let us film there—a tiny indication of the corruption supposedly rampant throughout Russian society. Consistent with events so far, it hasn't yet arrived, so he's refusing to open up. My trailer hasn't shown up either, so I change chez Alexander and discover his guilty secret—it's even more full of chocolate than mine.

A sexy, sweater-filling policewoman—their answer to our TV cop-show sirens—helps us with our work. She presents a glamorous contrast to the old stereotypes and is exactly what I imagined when I originally suggested a woman playing one of the police roles. Our first shot is in a dingy cell, reminding me of how prominently jails have figured in Russian culture, and of all the great minds, such as Solzhenitsyn, who have served time in them. In a bizarre case of Soviet nostalgia, certain jails have now become tourist haunts with inmates paying to be locked up and abused by the guards. On our last visit we dined in a restaurant decorated with documents, uniforms, and other detritus of the former state. Who could have anticipated the most bizarre example of this *nostalgie de la boue,* the elevation of the ugly, inefficient East German Trabby car into a symbol of contemporary chic. What's next—the gulag transformed into a holiday camp?

Jeff tells me that the delay has a positive aspect, enabling the police to eject the cell's three previous occupants and, fortunately, deodorize the place. Incarcerated inside, I have a good scene with a Russian actor with a wonderful toothless, leathery countenance who plays a drunken inmate. We have an incomprehensible exchange, mostly centered on his demand for a cigarette and my lack of one. This is followed by several interrogation scenes with Alexander and they all play well, despite the cacophony blasting from an open-air rock concert just down the street—just one of the four thousand shows playing this weekend.

After all the action scenes, it's a relief to play dialogue and subtle situations and to indulge in—dare I say it—a little acting. Alexander and I have filmed enough that our characters are now well established and familiar. We have both reached that much anticipated moment that happens in every movie when the situation reverses and the character starts playing the actor.

I offer to do some guerrilla filmmaking tonight so that we can set the fugitive Roger Chambers against the backdrop—and the stupendous production values—of the festivities. There's apparently going to be a light show in Red Square and it would be a coup to combine sightseeing with cinema. But, having started late, filming inexorably finishes even later. Making me promise to use my bodyguard in the streets tomorrow, Alexander mentions that Mr. Luzhkov has invited us to his Mayor's Cup show jumping event.

Sunday lives up to its name—a rare radiance dazzles the white linen breakfast tables. That cloud seeding has been a triumph! Later that afternoon, the Alexander duo pick me up at the hotel to drive to the Mayor's Cup event, and we walk through thronging crowds to get to the car. Our route takes us to a park by a distant bend in the river, on the way skirting hills with trees and lovely stretches of water. This city continues to surprise. Passing the parliamentary White House, both Alexanders surprise me further by saying they were there on that historic day in 1991 when Yeltsin quelled the antireformist backlash. I must get Sasha drunk and find out more. He has a cold. Producing a movie, not to mention acting in it, is surely an unremitting assault on the body's defenses.

The equine event is set in an open-air stadium. Escorted to our covered seats, we are greeted with the traditional bread, salt, and vodka. I also request hot tea—after all, it is that time of day— even though a lavish lunch, as belated as its movie counterpart, is about to be served. We then watch horses and riders compete in the sunlit paddock. This, our program tells us, is a fairly new event for modern Russia, although in 1913 it had led the world in horse breeding. Such private enterprise not being compatible with Soviet mores, the sport of kings never became the sport of comrades. Now it's in full revival, making up for those lost years of luxury and elegance. We all look like models in an advertisement for Polo clothes or expensive watches.

Requested for some press and TV interviews, I'm now attuned to such charming chicanery. Besides it's all very relaxing here, especially in the renewed, unfamiliar warmth. The glossily groomed thoroughbreds are a joy to behold, and we are so close to the course that we hear their dramatic snorts and thuds as they make the turn. The Mayor, however, fails to appear for his own Cup. On this day of all days he must be wanted in a thousand places. One of these is a reception tonight to which, Alexander announces, we are also invited. The triumph of hope over experience, I agree to go.

Back at the hotel, however, I take a nap and, weighed down by this week's worth of late nights, find that I can't wake up. Reluctantly I cancel tonight's invitation, even though I would have liked to congratulate Mayor Luzhkov on all he has achieved for his city. I think back on the last time Pat and I were face-to-face with a Russian politician. We had been invited to the Duma, the drab office building near the National, to meet with a leading Yeltsinite. Seated behind a desk as large as his ego and quaffing Coca-Cola, in between our remonstrations he launched into an anti-American tirade centered on the conduct of U.S. forces in the Balkan war then taking place. His bizarre parting gift to us was a CD of ballads sung by our bellicose host, whose marriage, ironically, failed apparently because he spent too much time watching American movies.

The TV news carries a report of another local triumph—a Russian has won the Golden Lion at the Venice Film Festival. Andrei Zvyagintsev's victory for his first effort, *The Return,* is tinged with sadness as its young leading actor drowned after the movie was completed—in the very same lake where the story was filmed. But it's wonderful to learn that, in the line of Andrei Tarkovsky and Nikita Mikhalkov, great work of international stature is again coming out of Russia.

Russian TV commercials, incidentally, are still less graphic than their U.S. counterparts, which seem only to reflect an overconsuming society that is either grossly overweight, sexually dysfunctional, or gastrically challenged. Significantly, liquor is not advertised on Russian airwaves, which probably explains why one of our film's backers is a vodka company. These commercials are a fertile training ground for a whole new generation of film directors and technicians who, like their colleagues in the West, use advertising to learn visual shorthand and how to connect with an audience.

There is also a report on another drama in the making. Among the candidates declaring for the parliamentary elections on December 7 are two politicians of diametrically opposed views. Anatoly Chubais is the controversial engineer of the country's post-Soviet mass privatization while Vladimir Zhirinovsky, wanting to stem that reformist tide, preaches a rabid, reactionary nationalism. Although the country's GNP is growing by 5 percent a year, its wealth is held by a handful of people. Stagnation looms unless this is shared among the 140 million other citizens. But at least there are now political parties to choose from. Vladimir Putin, meanwhile, rises above it all on his ever widening platform of popularity, seemingly assured of being returned to office—although I read elsewhere that a quarter of all Russians would vote for Stalin if he were running for president!

Шесть · 6

Placement, Placement, Placement

A thimbleful of experience is worth a tubful of knowledge.
— RUSSIAN PROVERB

Monday. As if on some cosmic cue, the rain has returned as we retreat one final time to Tsaritsino. The cloud bombers must be grounded. But at least the duel has been resolved and Richard has gone to his next movie. Today we are filming in a tiny cottage on the estate grounds. Its owner is astonished at seeing her modest yet spotless home invaded by a relentless, mud-tramping, sandwich-chomping, loud-speaking horde. The last time so many people were in her house, she says, was twenty years ago for her wedding. It is cramped but relatively cozy. Outside in the downpour the temperature has plunged to the forties. Someone remarks that they are getting their November in September. Maybe this is why Russia has become the leading country for suicides. Even John Aronson's sunny disposition has been eclipsed by a cold, and he goes about his work bundled up like the Michelin man.

Alexander's movie grandfather is being played by the veteran actor Aleksandr Belyavsky. Silver-haired and popular on TV,

Aleksandr informs me—and I believe him—that he will be drinking real vodka in our lengthy upcoming scene, in which he proposes multiple toasts over endless games of chess. But—surely only a minor production problem among so many—Aleksandr doesn't care for our sponsor's vodka. It's good to work with a scene-stealing old pro, and between us we manage to improvise some funny moments. The day goes well, perhaps because of the vodka; with consummate acting skill, I only pretend to slug it back. It's a talent that has served me well, most recently at a film festival in Kazakhstan. Lunching in a yurt tent on the remote steppe, I was served the eyes of a sheep as a special honor and managed to preserve international relations by faking enthusiastic chomping and swallowing.

The daily calls to California are demanding frequent purchases of phone cards, and I rush off to buy another before the next morning's pickup. Apparently I chose the wrong provider. There's one company whose signal is so powerful that calls can be made deep down in the subway. I'm reminded of rumors that the Soviets kept their empire subdued by zapping comrades with low pulsed microwaves, and that U.S. embassy staff in Moscow had been sickened by them. Before the collapse of the system, both Pat and I sensed the presence of a strange, depressing energy in several Communist bloc countries.

En route to the set, my newly energized phone shrills. It is Jeff informing me that he is stuck outside our café location. Despite the owner's previous consent, the place is locked, and permission to film has been withdrawn. Obviously their promised fax machine also failed to arrive. A proverb that I once had to intone playing that KGB agent comes mockingly to mind: "To live a life is not as easy as to cross a field." It sounds especially meaningful with a thick Russian accent. While Jeff and his location manager hunt for an alternative, I make another of those U-turns back to the hotel and use the time to order flowers for Pat's show.

A few hours later, we try again. Jeff has found a new place to film—a typical Moscow street, Kutuzov, west of the city. It's named after the marshall who faced down Napoleon at the bloody battle of Borodino, where 100,000 men died in one day. The event was memorably depicted in Sergei Bondarchuk's epic film version of *War and Peace.* Seemingly half the Soviet army was recruited to reenact this crucial historical turning point. It is reputed to be the most expensive movie ever made.

Bondarchuk also directed *Waterloo,* produced by the great Dino de Laurentiis. It was at the De Laurentiis studios, just south of Rome, that *The Shrew* was tamed in my film debut. Dino's entrepreneurial brilliance was evident in the cunning way visitors to his office were detoured by way of some seductive plans for his forthcoming *Waterloo* so that, by the time they reached his door, potential investors were frantic to be involved.

This new location even has one of the Seven Sisters towering, like a cross between a castle and cathedral, in the background. Moreover, in the delay, the rain has slackened, producing a low-wattage sun and an energetic, cloudy sky. The weather improves as the day progresses, until a golden light, as bright as an icon's halo, illuminates the action. The scene is one in which—constituting any tourist's worst nightmare—I'm handcuffed and bundled into a police car.

The street is full of high-end shops and boutiques, and our café location has metamorphosed into a large kiosk selling such luxuries as caviar, foie gras, and chocolate. It also stocks videos and DVDs, and Alexander treats me to the Russian version—hopefully not pirated—of *Cabaret.* Adapting our dialogue, we successfully shoot the scene, feeling blessed that that other assistant director, fate, forced us into using this much more atmospheric venue.

The next day, September 10, is when I was originally booked to return home. Instead, I fly there electronically, vicariously sharing Pat's LA life. She tells me that the upper gallery of the Academy—she is the first photographer to have been granted exhibition space on both floors—has now been hung. The show would normally have opened tomorrow, a Thursday, but because that is the anniversary of the 9/11 atrocity, the following day is chosen.

Pat has just returned from a party for an old friend, Giorgio Armani. "And how was he?" I inquire. "I've no idea," comes the reply. "The music was so loud it made conversation impossible! We just screamed at each other." Noise has become an international nuisance. I'm reminded of when I served as honorary chairman of the international Rebuild Dubrovnik Fund and learned that one of the most intolerable assaults on the city came when the enemy trained large loudspeakers on the city and blasted it with Serbian rock music.

Today we are filming in an apartment belonging to the parents of Vlad, the young assistant director and my former minder. Apparently they are away, so he's giving us the run of his elegant, spacious digs, notable for some newly decorated art nouveau details and interesting city views. Here no one bothers to wear felt booties on the gleaming parquet floor. Do the absent owners know about their son's largesse and our invasion, or is it rather like that film *Risky Business,* where young Tom Cruise showed similar entrepreneurial acumen? Apartment prices in Moscow have apparently risen 30 percent in one year, so perhaps this is just a useful source of extra income.

Things have come a long way since 1963, when Pat was first in Moscow researching her story for *Glamour* magazine. Taken to a "typical" apartment, she was entertained by the resident family. On leaving and discovering she had left something behind, she returned, only to find that three other families had already moved back in.

There are the usual delays—and not just because of the time it takes to haul cables, crew, and equipment to an upper floor. Jeff dislikes the dress Maria is wearing and requests something sexier. We are also having another product placement timeout as the family's rather stylish TV is replaced with an ugly, bulky one provided by yet another sponsor. They had tried to install it in the grandfather's modest cottage set, but agreed it looked ludicrously out of place there. No doubt it will make an appearance elsewhere. Although Russia is caught in the middle of huge commercial upheavals, time here is definitely not money—yet.

There's a great deal of hacking and coughing from the many crew members who, like most of their European peers, are smokers. I read that over 60 percent of Russian men smoke and I wonder if that teetotaling martial arts disciplinarian, Vladimir Putin, abstains from this vice. Young people puff away as if they are immortal—and without permission or apology. But today's barking, wheezing, and sneezing is also the cumulative result of all those late, wet nights.

Compensating for this—and no doubt exacerbating the situation—craft service, the pretentious showbiz term for caterer on set, has gone into caloric overdrive. Declining the violently pink salami sandwich, I'm given a whole chocolate cherry cake to eat, plus three Snickers bars. This turns out to be providential, as we wait until 5:30 P.M. for what they still call lunch to be served. I think of filming in the United States, where stiff financial penalties are meted out to any who transgress the inflexible mealtime rules. But at least things here have come a long way from the simple fare, the soups, boiled eggs, and pickles, that seemed to be the staple when filming in former Iron Curtain countries.

Katrina has rushed home and found a little black dress that not only fits Maria but also passes Jeff's sex appeal test. "Action!" is finally called. Katrina is proving invaluable, having become another essential link between the nationalities. A theater student at the Vakhtangov, she tells me that the entire course is costing her only $4,000—an absolute bargain. And certainly the hands-on training she is getting on the movie will be invaluable. No doubt she'll go far, and I'll look for her name. I remember working on other films with similar bright young assistants who now run Hollywood studios and production companies.

The following day brings the second anniversary of the 9/11 assault on America. Russian opinion appears divided. Initial sympathy seems to have given way to a more world-weary skepticism, some seeing it as the catalyst of yet another round in the old international "Great Game," distinguished this time by a new gung-ho American unilateralism. Few believe that George W. Bush's foray into the Middle East will be temporary, and they urge the rebuilding of a more authoritarian Great Russia to counterbalance such potential hegemony. Meanwhile, some of the democratic freedoms won under Yeltsin have been trimmed in the name of greater security—the same reason used to justify the U.S. Patriot Act's suspension of some constitutional liberties. I wonder what chauvinistic euphemism Putin will use to cover his aggrandizing actions.

The skies are clear and sunny—just as they were on that fateful day over New York and Washington. Robert and I drive out through the suburbs, Mercedes giving way to Ladas, concrete high-rises to wooden dachas, and at last we arrive at a lovely lake—apparently part of the Moscow River—where a huge floating boat hotel is moored. This location was only found this morning, and from a tourist brochure! Taking advantage of the scenery and the sunshine, Jeff decides to film the encounter between Robert, me, and the petty crook Oleg, formerly scripted as inside his apartment, on a boat in the middle of the lake. We require only a skeleton crew, so most of the unit remain supine on shore, catching some rare rays. Filming on water is notoriously difficult, but the skies and winds remain placid and everything goes well.

We shoot nonstop until twilight's last gleaming. "Lunch" is this time served at 8:30 P.M. and wolfed down, the fresh air having whipped up ravenous appetites. That evening I feel chilly and can't warm up. I just hope I haven't caught the virus that's been going around. Perhaps it's due to rare sunspot activity after spending so much of the day outside.

The boat hotel's huge restaurant is taken over for the second encounter between Oleg and me. Perhaps because of my growing feverishness, the scene in which I reluctantly trade my son's ring for a handgun has a heated intensity. Afterward, returned to my luxuriously landlocked hotel, I parboil myself in a hot bath but still feel shivery when the light is finally switched off at that graveyard hour, four in the morning.

Only moments later, it seems, I'm woken by the sun pouring bloodily through the red blinds. My cold, though, seems no better, and I order that old stand-by, chicken soup. Later gargling with salt water, I curse myself for indulging in the previous sweet weeks of cake and candy and ignoring the healthy, freshly squeezed juices also available at the hotel's huge breakfast buffet.

Picked up in the early afternoon, we barge our way out west through choked weekend traffic to the Sparrow Hills. Here, from a bluff above another long, lazy loop in the Moscow River, is a spectacular view over the sunlit city, with the Novodevichy Convent gleaming like a Fabergé trinket in the distance. To the back of us soar the Stalinist spires of Moscow University: it's a spectacular spot for filming. The only problem is that everyone seems to be in agreement, and it's crowded with tourists and Muscovites alike. Bridal groups pose, couples promenade, children play, balloons hover, refreshments are sold and souvenirs briskly traded, while above the babble, a brass band booms. It looks like a lively panoramic Repin painting come startlingly alive.

In a key scene with Alexander, while still handcuffed together, we strike a deal delaying my imminent deportation. This requires a certain subtlety—we can't just yell at each other to be heard. All imprecations for quiet are ignored; in fact, they make things worse. The band, realizing that there might be financial inducement in their silence, plays even louder. In the same vein, an angry merchant shouts at us for disrupting business, loudly dismissing our polite suggestion that we might be actually attracting it. Exploding fireworks only add to the chaos. Eventually we give up, reluctantly deciding to rerecord this dialogue in the looping session back in LA. I don't object, as I have always found these occasions to be opportunities for further creativity.

There are the usual delays. The handcuffs don't fit, and the police van, from which we are supposed to be filming the passing scene, is too big for its tow trailer. But I'm now as fatalistic as a Russian. Besides, for once the sun stays out, and the relaxed, festive spirit is infectious. I take some photos with my Swedish throwaway, which looks slightly ridiculous amid all the competing digital gadgetry. A bride and groom ask Alexander and me to pose with them for good luck—ours as much as theirs, I hope.

Inevitably the golden light fades, and we are forced to film the van interiors while stationary in a dark parking lot. John lights the windows to brilliantly simulate daylight, the van is rocked and rolled, moving shadows are cast, and we are off. Except, it being Saturday night, every Moscow Vin Diesel has gathered outside, competing to see how loudly they can rev up their motorcycles and hotrods, while gangsta rap music shreds the air.

We struggle to the end of the scene. My handkerchief has become my most important prop, as my nose is now running faster than the film through our camera. Thank goodness I'm meant to look a little rough at this stage. Driving away at the end of work, I see that a full moon has replaced the balloons in a bright sky. The spires of Moscow University are lit up like one of those Disneyesque enchanted castles. It's hard to believe that this romantic extravaganza is reputed to have been built with slave labor. Sleep comes intermittently because of a violently sore throat.

I croak home at daylight, anxious to find out how Pat's exhibition opening went last night. *Imaging and Imagining* is a smash success. Over eight hundred people attended, and word of mouth is positive. As for my world of imaging, the morning finds us guerrilla filmmaking down in the Metro, where it's normally forbidden or permits have to be obtained. I've done this kind of cheeky, smash-and-grab shooting before, notably once in the streets of Jerusalem's Orthodox quarter with a camera concealed in a van, and another time in Venice on the Grand Canal, where we would stop off at a photogenic palazzo or vista, quickly play the scene, and move on one step ahead of the *polizia*.

You can only pull off this kind of stunt with a small, maneuverable crew, and today we have the bare minimum. As well as controlling the light, John is operating the camera, toting it around on his broad, competent shoulders. The rest of us meld with the real passengers, so it's probably just as well that Alexander is not present in his scary cop's uniform. There are no calls for action—just discreet hand signals—but no one seems to even notice us, let alone look in the camera. Our prepared story in case of trouble is that we are film students from California, but fortunately this improbable alibi is never required. With an unwitting cast of hundreds, we shoot some wonderful scenes on escalators and platforms. At one point, with a vestige of that "in the moment" madness that sent me scaling lofty buildings as the spirited D'Artagnan, I risk boarding a train, jumping off again just before the doors closed to transport me irretrievably off the set.

Filming continues on the plaza atop the underground shopping mall opposite the National Hotel. Denied permission to film in Red Square itself, our shot of St. Basil's Cathedral and Lenin's tomb sandwiched between the State Historical Museum and the Kremlin walls says it all: we were definitely there! I'm so pleased with this outcome. Then we film inside the hotel itself. I'm relieved, as I'm feeling increasingly unwell, my torrential nose making speaking difficult. But the show must, and does, go on in one of the hotel suites. It's next door to mine, so I'm grateful to lie down between takes. My nose seems as red as one of the Soviet stars that used to adorn the sunlit buildings in the background. Slightly feverish, I find my imagination to be similarly overheated. Nevertheless, the work is enjoyable. It has been a good day, although I'm thankful when we pull the plugs early—just before midnight.

Alexander offers some tickets to Mussorgsky's *Khovanschina* at the Bolshoi tomorrow, our free day. Pat and I are huge opera buffs, and this is one that neither of us has seen. Can I pull myself together enough to go, as I so much want to, or should I concentrate on getting better? By morning, the constant drip, drip, drip subsides, revealing a raw, red throat. All my homeopathic standbys, so reliable over the past thirty years, are inadequate—even chicken soup seems useless. Fortunately it's a day off, and finding myself still yawning, I yield gratefully because I know sleep is where the healing process is really enabled.

A fitful nap is interrupted by a loud noise. For a feverish, dream-drenched moment I imagine Rasputin is bursting in to heal me. But it turns out to be Whitney, our amiable assistant director, calling to say that he's suffering from the same symptoms. He went to the American hospital and was diagnosed with a serious infection. Having taken an antibiotic shot, he already feels better and offers to come round and drop off some of his pills and sprays. On his arrival, we discuss our mutual symptoms as well as the substantial amount of work that remains. I assure him I will be there tomorrow, assuming I can stand upright.

Reluctant to use drugs, I still hope to cure myself with rest and alternative means. That evening, watching a TV program about Mozart, I'm horrified to learn that he died with some of the same symptoms I have, especially a raging sore throat. I'm relieved, however, that along with his genius, I lack his swollen joints—so far.

Magic Hour

Regardless of how long you may make a rope,
it will always have an end.
— RUSSIAN PROVERB

Next morning, I decide to bite the bullet—or at least a powerful pill—and go to the hospital. Sickness helped defeat both Napoleon and Hitler, and I don't want to become another sad statistic. I took out medical insurance before coming to Russia, but true to Sod's Law, it has just expired. The ever-competent Katrina metamorphoses into nurse, arranging everything and accompanying me to the hospital on the way to today's location at Domodedovo Airport.

The American Medical Center is, to my relief, a thoroughly modern facility. After handing over my credit card—in faithful homage to the priorities of U.S. medical practice—I'm seen almost immediately by the same doctor who treated Whitney. I'm perversely proud when she announces that my infection is worse than his, amounting to an acute tonsillitis. Antibiotics are injected, as well as Alexander's hated steroids to reduce the inflammation, allowing me to speak and perform. Compromising deeply held medical principles is regrettable, but considering the work that lies ahead, with a long flight in two days' time, I can't afford to be too scrupulous. The doctor only requests a signed photo in return for saving me, which I promise to send. Then we race for the airport.

Domodedovo, on the fringe of the city where the superrich are beginning to bulldoze the forests to build their megamansions, has been transformed since the last time Pat and I arrived there on that flight from Sochi. It's now as gleamingly modern as the hospital. My trailer is stationed just outside the departure hall, and the day is punctuated with a litany of flight information, allowing me to travel vicariously to such alluring destinations as Tomsk, Baku, Minsk, Perm, Vladivostok, Novosibirsk, and Astrakhan. Russia has some 237 airlines, and they all seem very busy. Domestic flight is much safer than it was twenty years ago, when obsolete 1960s-era air traffic control equipment was still in use, and the U.S. State Department issued a directive discouraging its employees from flying internally on Russian airlines.

We are filming in the airport's nursery, one end of which has been transformed into our movie set café, with planes seen coming and going through its large windows. Opposite, exhausted mothers with fretful children listlessly watch us play. This final scene—my farewell to Alexander—has been scheduled in the right place, at the end of the movie. Often the last scene of a movie is filmed first, usually with an unrehearsed script, requiring both imagination and flexibility. Now there's a comfortable familiarity—we've all shared a great deal, both in the story and in real life. At one point, Alexander's hero, Arnold Schwarzenegger, is mentioned. Deciding to take a chance, I improvise a line that refers to him as "the politician." Time, and the California electorate, will tell if this educated guess makes the final cut!

Before losing the light, we grab some shots on the platform of the sleek new bullet train that whisks passengers to the city center in a mere forty-five minutes. This gleaming efficiency contrasts with our ritual two-hour wait—this time for props. We use it to discuss a possible location for Alexander's final confrontation with the hoodlum, Oleg. What aspect of Moscow have we still not shown? I suggest the *banya,* or bathhouse, as my guidebook claims that "you can't say you've really been to Russia unless you've visited one." The location manager is sent off to investigate.

Eventually we continue filming, by now late at night. The scene is our arrival and—hopefully my dress rehearsal for the day after tomorrow—our departure through passport control. Katya, Alexander's lovely wife, playing the immigration officer, is the perfect representative of the new-style smiling welcome for visitors.

The next morning I feel much worse, probably a result of the drugs as much as anything. Going to breakfast, I pass Henry Kissinger on the stairs. He was once my opponent in a paddle tennis tournament at a mutual friend's home in Acapulco, and his furiously aggressive will to win was as impressive as his off-court affability. How did he function when he felt under the weather on his many epoch-shaping foreign trips? I remember John Foster Dulles confessing on his retirement that he had mishandled too many situations because of jetlag. Now I'm simply too groggy to stop, engage, and possibly bother my old tennis adversary.

I haven't checked my e-mail for two days, and I find a cache of 120 messages demanding notice. I'll wait until I'm home. Home! After a time, no matter how luxurious the hotel or rewarding the work, that irresistible domestic siren song begins to sound. I once heard an eighty-year-old Graham Greene claim in a BBC interview that he had "been to too many places to be happy." It's time to be "in residence" for a spell, and finally it no longer seems improbable that I will be in my own bed tomorrow night.

Today's filming is the chase scene, originally written for cars but now transposed to the Moscow River, alongside which our little wayfaring collection of vans and trucks is parked. Happily, the weather forecast for rain was wrong. It's sunny but chilly by the water. We concentrate on filming a shot of our wicked lady, Maria, still alarmingly underdressed and surrounded by a bevy of gangsters, as they make off down the river. Then, swathed in protective layers of T-shirts, I join Alexander and a real police officer in his sleek launch for our "martini shot," the final one of the day.

John heroically straps himself and his camera to the prow of the launch like an oversized figurehead, and with blue siren light flashing, we cast off. The city, burnished by a fiery setting sun, looks spectacular from this low angle. Like a speeded-up résumé of my whole visit, we zoom along under the Kremlin walls, passing the landmarks that have become endearingly familiar. Peter is indeed great as he looms over us in his fantasy steel rigging, Gorky Park is no more than a green streak. We break every rule of navigation, zigzagging from bank to bank like drunken sailors. Conversation is impossible in the wind and noise, so Alexander and I dramatically point and gesture. Perhaps we'll be able to add something more coherent when the film is looped, but I already hear an exciting score playing over this chase. It is exhilarating—and a perfect way to wind down my work on the film. Then it's all over.

Back on shore, we have applause, speeches, and toasts. Dear comrades embrace, and Alexander presents me with a tin of caviar. I present Nazar with my picnic hamper. I'm grateful for his constant kindness, attentiveness, and discretion—I hope he will now treat himself to some of the gastronomic pleasures he lavished on me. There's a TV news crew in attendance, and now I have a pertinent and informed response to the question I was asked on arrival at Sheremetyevo, "How do you like filming in Russia?" After a farewell *do svidaniya*, I'm driven back to the hotel for the last time at "magic hour," so beloved of cinematographers, when day suffuses into night. The romantic French have the *mot juste* for this kind of light—*entre chien et loup*: when you can't distinguish a dog from a wolf.

There's the same feeling at the end of every movie—a curious blend of relief and regret. Some even assert that the real filmmaking starts now, when the disparate pieces so painstakingly accumulated are equally patiently put together, in the hope that the resulting assembly will amount to more than the sum of its parts. After thawing and unwinding in a bath, I slowly pack away the jumbled memories and belongings accumulated over the past fifty memorable days.

My end is my beginning. Vlad, who evidently was not banished from the family film set, comes to pick me up in the white limo for the return to Sheremetyevo. Like Gaev in *The Cherry Orchard*, I make a fond farewell to my room before Sasha arrives to give me an official producer's send-off. Finally and legitimately on "road to airport," I'm curious to see if the cityscape has changed in the intervening weeks.

Certainly I have changed, possessing a deeper understanding of the people in the streets of this Janus-faced city, where businessmen rub shoulders with beggars, modernism coexists with medievalism, and many ancient buildings are brand-new. I'm only sorry that there was no opportunity to travel farther afield and see if Moscow's prosperity has trickled down to the rest of the country. Have we been in a glorious goldfish bowl here? We pass the monument commemorating the place where the Nazi advance was stopped by Marshall Zhukov, allowing that old ally, winter, to pick off the retreating forces. Now who can hold back the advancing invasion of capitalist consumerism?

The stygian airport VIP waiting room is already fogged with smoke that's not exactly balm to my sore throat, but tobacco-intolerant California is only hours away. Vlad insists on sitting out the wait with me, so we talk in an enforced, desultory way whenever his cell phone is silent. In a final flourish of bureaucracy, I register money on one last form. I remember all too vividly the experience of an art dealer friend on his first visit to Russia. On leaving the country, he failed to report the funds he was carrying on behalf of a St. Petersburg gallery. Thrown into a cell and refused permission to make a phone call, he was only saved by the airline, which paid for his release.

Eventually there's a familiar sound, a lady announcer calling flights—but this time mine. There is no suspicious soldier scrutinizing passport photographs at the airplane door, as in former days. In a final illustration of the new international business ethic, the Aeroflot plane turns out to be a familiar Boeing 767. Its video monitor announces that we have 9,767 nonstop kilometers to Los Angeles as we take off into another rainstorm—the brief, blessed Indian summer appears to be over.

Passing Murmansk, so potent with wartime memories of Allied convoys and an earlier instance of international cooperation, we cross over to Greenland and on and on—and on. I watch Madonna in a movie that isn't very good, despite the armies of assistants, personal trainers, chefs, and ballroom-size trailers that were no doubt on hand, even though the film is set on a desert island. It comes as a forceful reminder of how fiendishly difficult it is to triumph in this impossible-to-pin-down, will-o'-the-wisp medium. Success is attained as much by luck as judgment, and the rules and rewards change constantly. What on earth, I wonder, have we managed to capture on all that celluloid running at twenty-four frames a second through our mono-magazine camera?

It's still magic hour outside when we land in Los Angeles, and I head for home through the strange streets of an unfamiliar city.

PART THREE

Lights

Gollywood star!

Gollywood Actor

The sole substitute for an experience which we have
not ourselves lived through is art and literature.
— ALEXANDER SOLZHENITSYN

There follows a week of opening letters, erasing amassed
e-mail, enjoying married life and Alexander's caviar, and
catching up on sleep and domestic chores. The antibiotics run
their stern course, and in about ten days I feel fully recovered.
Pat's exhibition, finally visited, more than lives up to its burgeoning reputation.

Enjoying our usual Sunday morning walk in the astonishing urban wilderness of Franklin Canyon, just twenty blocks from that
gilded GUM equivalent, Rodeo Drive, we pass two people speaking a now familiar language. Greeting them with a cheery *dobroye
utro*, they ask how I know Russian, and I respond that I was just
there. "And how was it?" I confirm how prosperous things look.
"Yes, none of our Russian friends want to come here any more because they have everything there. Besides, you have to work too
hard in the USA!"

In early October, Robert Madrid returns to LA and calls with an account of the final days of filming. He tells of hovering in a large military helicopter and blowing up our villain in a smaller model one. Problems persisted. The crucial shot of our heroes leaving the helicopter was only grabbed at the very last moment, as a high-ranking official had unexpectedly come to the airport to put paratroopers through their paces, thus shutting down all other activity for most of the day. But we finally made it: Truffaut's battered, oft delayed and misdirected conveyance eventually reached its destination.

John and Whitney have gone for a few days of well-earned vacation to St. Petersburg, at last spending close-up time with their partners. Both Jeff and Gib Jaffe stayed on in Moscow and are back at work editing. Having now seen all the dailies, they report that the work has a strange, compelling quality.

The newspapers are full of articles about Russia—or maybe they were always there, but my focus on them was not quite so engaged. Pat, *à la recherche du temps perdu*, buys thick peasant bread, blinis, and caviar in one of the many expatriate Russian stores in West Hollywood. Back at the Academy, we run into Whitney, who reports having seen a rough cut of our film, attesting equally mysteriously that "it has its own logic and amusing quality."

At the Directors Guild I host a memorial service for my good and much lamented friend, the film director John Schlesinger. Among his distinguished body of films that are recalled is a particular favorite of mine, *An Englishman Abroad,* recounting the experience of the actress Coral Browne playing Shakespeare in Moscow at the height of the Cold War. At the end of one performance, the notorious English spy Guy Burgess rushed into her dressing room and threw up in her washbasin, thus initiating an improbable friendship. My service as an English diplomat in Russia was, I trust, a little more decorous. I'm uncertain, though, that I would have passed the Cambridge spies' test for acceptance into their treacherous profession. Apparently Kim Philby was horrified when informed that I might play him in a film about his treasonous life. "But he's not a gentleman," he protested.

Concorde takes its last commercial flight. I would have welcomed the use of such globe-shrinking transportation when, learning later of my mother's death, I arrange to fly back to England for her funeral. The plane, however, unprecedentedly breaks down, and no other travel option could get me there in time. It almost seems as if my mother is in some way behind this—so typically self-denying, and so reluctant to be intrusive or demanding. Instead, I wake at the same hour as her service and, surrounding myself with her photographs, meditate on this extraordinary bond—like the one that predicates the action in our movie—that parents and children seem never to lose, despite all temporal and physical distances.

I accept a guest-starring role in an enormously popular TV series made in a local studio. But acting there is like working in a boring factory, churning out a predictable, marketable product like wallpaper. There's none of the scary sense of flying by the seat of the pants into unknown realms that characterized our recent film—and I miss it. Noel Coward's assertion that "television is for being on, not for watching" is invalidated.

At the beginning of November, the showbiz newspaper *Variety* publishes a huge photograph of Alexander and me handcuffed together, along with a congratulatory message from Sasha Izotov and Czar Pictures on the completion of principal photography. My co-star finally returns to his adopted country and calls me. Despite jet lag, he sounds very upbeat. He's also pleased to be back in the sunshine as—to keep the meteorological record straight—it has turned very cold in Russia.

When we eventually get together, he gives me—as is the custom of his country—a little present. This endearing gesture is repeated at every subsequent encounter, and I am now the proud owner of a tiny musical Kremlin, a porcelain double eagle, and a miniature samovar. Pat tells me that when she was in Russia in the less affluent 1960s, she rarely had an encounter without being given some token, whether it was a piece of fruit or a flower.

There's also a reunion with Jeff and Gib, both now returned from the eastern front, in their far west Santa Monica editing suite. For the first time, I view the results of our labors. Now cut down to eighty-nine minutes, the movie certainly moves. Even on the tiny screen, it looks very promising.

In December, with Muscovites earning three times the national average and after cannily topping up retirees' pensions, Mayor Luzhkov is overwhelmingly reelected to a third term. In the new year, Sasha Izotov comes to LA for the Golden Globe Awards, the first of many glitzy, self-reverential ceremonies, where the idea for our film was born. We meet for dinner and reminiscences and, of course, renewed vodka toasts. I recount how I once played a Russian who came to Los Angeles in search of fame and fortune, but found it in a downtown factory making sex toys. This was in Len Richmond's cheeky independent film *A Dirty Little Business*. Based on a true story, it was made on a minuscule budget in a real factory that, in addition to dildos and bondage leather gear, produced kosher love potions! The great Brian Cox was also in the cast, using the Russian he acquired teaching at the Moscow Art Theater.

In mid-February, Alexander shows me a tape of *Moscow Heat*— finished apart from the musical score and sound effects. I'm impressed, although the emphasis seems to have shifted somewhat from the drama to the action, no doubt as a result of Tony Leung's showy contribution. Some of the product placements, to put it mildly, are obvious and repetitive. Even though the James Bond film *Tomorrow Never Dies* also featured vodka and cell phone brands—along with six other products—their placement managed to be a little less blatant.

There have been some clever editorial ideas. Alexander's long interrogation scene of the wounded Robert in the hospital has been cut into several sections placed throughout the film, so that the information slowly accumulated adds to the growing suspense. I can see where some equally creative looping, combined with a judicious score, could really embellish what we have. Alexander tells me that the premiere is planned for August.

Vladimir Putin is swept back into office with a huge majority of about 80 percent. There are television images of him repossessing his gilded Kremlin, walking in solitary triumph down the red carpet like some latter-day Napoleon. Like the Corsican tyrant, he seems to have fostered a new spirit of national optimism, reflected in the rising birthrate, a timely correction to one of his major concerns. There is also news of a nuclear suitcase bomb in Pakistan, making our film seem not only relevant, but also prescient—especially as enough material is apparently missing from Russia to make many dirty bombs.

At the beginning of April, just before the looping session, I take another long look at the film and make more suggestions. These are then put into place at LA's Millennium Sound Studios. The session is a joy, a truly collaborative experience. I encourage both the sound editor and the engineer, as well as Robert Madrid—there sporting his co-producer's hat—to contribute as many ideas as possible, and together we make significant improvements. Extra dialogue is sneaked in over long shots and when heads are turned. I especially relish restoring my character's initial refusal of a gun at our lakeside encounter with Oleg and adding relevant dialogue over one of the more egregious vodka bottle shots to help justify its inclusion. At the end of the session everyone seems to share my upbeat response.

Next to record is Richard Tyson, who arrives neatly suited and unremarkably coiffed from church, while incongruously parroting aloud the Russian for "I have to take a piss" that Alexander has just phoned through to him. Curiously, the film may be a little fashionably violent, but, following the dictates of our Russian producers, it is mostly free of profanity. I just hope that my "You bastard" makes the cut!

I learn that the film's international sales, especially at the imminent Cannes Film Festival, have been taken on by a company named Lightning Entertainment. Meanwhile at the current American Film Market held in Santa Monica, the movie trailer has attracted significant attention. It is also playing on the Internet, but my computer skills prove insufficient to access it.

The LA Pacific Design Center presents *Russian Nights: A Cultural Experience,* an exhibition dedicated to "preserving traditions and advancing contemporary arts and culture." Russian press and TV are also present and Alexander and I seize the opportunity to report positively on our film's progress toward release. In a gallery emblazoned with samples of exciting new art, I meet one of its organizers, Stas Namin. This brilliant composer, singer, musician, photographer, and all-round entrepreneur both documented and provoked—as with his pop group Flowers—the extraordinary cultural changes that turned his homeland upside down. There is now a National Center for Contemporary Art in Moscow, he tells me, with the prospect of it soon moving to a significant new building.

We spend May Day—once an occasion for the display of Russian military might in Red Square—in California's peaceful Napa Valley, where only ranks of vines parade across the scene. Pat and I are the guests of Serge and Tatiana Sorokko, two expatriate Russians. Serge, a prominent San Francisco gallery owner, will be mounting an exhibition of Pat's work in November, while his elegant wife is a correspondent for Russia's glossy new *Vogue* magazine. At a lunch there I meet Andrei Kozyrev, the influential minister of foreign affairs in the Yeltsin government, and we talk about the political changes he helped instigate. Another guest from Russia likens his country's postcommunist experience to falling into a well—and breaking both legs.

With Mikhail Khodorkovsky's continued detainment in Moscow on tax evasion charges, an economic squeeze on the oligarchs intensifies. Questions are asked about the hugely profitable construction contracts awarded to Mayor Luzhkov's wife, Elena Baturina, now reputed to be the nation's richest woman. Will Russia have its own Enron scandals, complete with handcuffed, humbled executives paraded publicly to inquests on their previously uninhibited activities? The country seems paused at a historic crossroad, debating over which path to take: returning to more authoritarian rule or preserving the constitutional freedoms forged out of the demise of the old repressive system only thirteen tumultuous years ago.

"I am happy to inform you that Lightning Entertainment sold 'Moscow Heat' in Cannes to 17 countries (and 5 more are very interested)!" an e-mail from Alexander announces. Just before Memorial Day, there is another message updating those countries to 31. A further progress report reveals that a new film trailer has helped sell the film to more territories, although many others are opting to delay their decision until the film is entirely finished and presented on the big screen. The movie's sound score, accumulated over sixty-four Hollywood tracks instead of the meager eight used in Moscow, has given it an added richness. Consistent, it seems, with the delays experienced while filming, the premiere of *Moscow Heat* is now postponed to September.

Девять · 9

On the Western Front

Facts don't exist until man puts into them something
of his own, a bit of free human genius—of myth.
— BORIS PASTERNAK

My present on Father's Day, June 20, is tickets for Pat and
me to Barcelona, where I film another flamboyant role in
a contemporary drama called *Crusader*. This time I'm a media
czar who—in what could be interpreted as a strange parallel with
Putin—squeezes the independent media for political purposes.
There is even talk of controlling the Internet, an issue that has
apparently been newly raised in the Kremlin. Also in the movie is
Richard Tyson—once more transformed with a beard and long
hair and again playing the villain—who arrives the day I leave.
There are the inevitable reminiscences about our Russian adventure and especially our dusty duel.

A Siberian siren, Maria Sharapova, wins at Wimbledon, continuing the work of Anna Kournikova to invalidate previous unkind
caricatures of Russian womanhood. At the same time, confirming

long-standing rumors, it is acknowledged that Lenin died of syph-
ilis. The propagator of a diseased dogma was himself sick in the
head, and his long-preserved body had already rotted within.
Meanwhile, in a move that would have amused the ruthless Lenin,
the embattled Khodorkovsky is forced to exchange his private jet
for a steel courtroom interrogation cage. His prosecution repre-
sents the thin edge of a potentially huge wedge. Though most are
quietly toeing the Putin line, there are now reported to be more
billionaires in Moscow than in New York.

On my return to Los Angeles, just a few days after Alexander's
birthday in mid-July, we meet again for lunch. He presents me
with another charming blue-and-white figurine—appropriately a
policeman—as well as the latest *Moscow Heat* news. Our film is
now completely finished; the work done thousands of miles apart
in Moscow and Los Angeles fortunately meshes, merges, and
matches up. The Russian distributor is Karo-Film, one of the most
innovative of the new breed of exhibitors. Plans for the Moscow
premiere have again been modified, our producers being reluctant
to release their film against too much competition from foreign
movies. They are seeking a "window" sometime in November. In
this same month the American Film Market, the largest in the
world and the self-styled "Home of the Independents," takes place
in Los Angeles, where Lightning Entertainment will be screening
the movie for potential foreign buyers.

The longer the delay, however, the more it seems our film will
benefit from the improving news about Russian cinema. As recently
as 1998 movie receipts amounted to only $8 million; in 2003 they
had boomed to $200 million, pushing the country to tenth in the
world box office stakes. Moreover, a new film, *Night Watch*—"our
answer to Tarantino," according to Nikita Mikhalkov—has bested
the blockbuster *Spiderman*, earning in its first few weeks of release
a staggering $12 million. A huge potential market for homemade

fare, if properly made and marketed, is proved to exist. Hoping to catch this rising, benevolent tide, Alexander is already considering a new action-themed script with Robert Madrid, to be filmed in the winter. "We now want to show *Moscow Snow,*" he enthuses.

Meanwhile, *Moscow Heat*'s new trailer, a kaleidoscope of energetic images, improves on its predecessor, even concluding with the improvised "Schwarzenegger the politician" quip. This only confirms that the lunatics must be occasionally unfettered and encouraged to play inside their madhouse. Actors should be free, without undue self-indulgence, to provide as much varied raw material for the editor as possible. One rewarding technique is for the director to allow another take after a scene has been recorded to the satisfaction of everyone involved. This tends to liberate the preoccupied imagination, producing unexpected riches.

At the beginning of August, another e-mail from Alexander trumpets: "I just got news from Izotov that we will have World Premiere in Moscow on November 24th at 'Pushkinsky'—the best movie theatre in Russia." Putin has apparently been invited.

Alexander comes to our house with Robert Madrid to film a little promotional piece for Russian television before returning to Moscow. We enthuse about the movie, filming against the background of the sunstruck city, our swimming pool, and a token palm tree, trusting that this will provide an appropriate illusion of Hollywood glamour. I'm impressed with Alexander's burgeoning savoir-faire as a producer. Promoting a film is as important as actually making it and often costs almost as much. Alexander is at least now firing his publicity cannons at a more appropriate time, when they are finally in close range of their objective.

What kind of Moscow will he find on his return? Newspaper articles lament the current "tearing down" of the city, even in such historic spots as Pushkin Square. The historic Manezh was accidentally burned down and the doomed Moskva is threatened with replacement by a facsimile. Leading architects from all over the world are lobbying Putin to halt such destruction and preserve the city's heritage. Can the right balance be achieved? Certainly London's buildings suffered as much from insensitive postwar planners as from Hitler's bombers.

Meanwhile, abandoning our own overheated city, Pat and I set off for cooler Aspen, Colorado, where I've been asked to perform at its summer music festival. I'm playing Dimitri Shostakovich in a powerful piece for two actors, two singers, a string quartet, and full orchestra called "Russian David . . . Soviet Goliath." It's centered around the long life-and-death struggle that developed between Shostakovich and Stalin after the latter saw the popularly acclaimed *Lady Macbeth of Mtsensk* and pronounced *nyet*. In a newspaper article he himself penned, headlined "Muddle Instead of Music," Stalin might have been describing himself when he dismissed the opera as "coarse, primitive, vulgar," with music that "quacks, grunts, and growls."

From then on, Shostakovich learned to sing in his political cage and wrote music that, while superficially conforming to the Great Teacher's standards, also served as his coded commentary on events. John Rubinstein plays the bluff, sinister tyrant, dismissing my agonized testimonial with that perceptive Russian saying, perhaps also pertinent to this narrative, "He lies like an eyewitness."

A lingering impression is Stalin's deadly pervasiveness in his role as the nation's ultimate cultural commissar. A great movie buff, he allowed no film to be made without his imprimatur on the script and personal censorship of the results. A great fan of Tarzan movies and westerns, he banned all excessive screen kissing. One of the most significant buildings in the Kremlin was his personal cinema, an active expression of Lenin's perceptive statement that "of all the arts, the most important for us is the cinema."

I wonder if Stalin would have approved the current hit film in Russia, *Night Watch*. *Variety* reports that it has broken the all-time Russian box office record held previously by *The Lord of the Rings*. After only five weeks, it has earned an astonishing $15 million. This is all the more remarkable as there are only four hundred cinemas in the country with a stiff ticket price of $5—exorbitant considering the average monthly wage is only $200.

The *Moscow Heat* website displays the film's poster, showing Alexander brooding in extreme close-up on a hot red background. Inexplicably, the hammer and sickle emblem appears in the artwork, presumably because this means "Russia" to most people, just as the Eiffel Tower says "France." The website can be accessed on Google. A Moscow native, Sergei Brin, launches this now indispensable resource he cofounded as a public company, becoming as rich as any of his contemporary oligarchs.

Russia's richest man, the secretive oil tycoon Roman Abramovich, has purchased a new Boeing 767, the plane that brought hundreds of us back from Russia, entirely for his own use. For the moment, this flying palace is far more impressive than Putin's aging Ilyushin presidential planes. In late August, two Ilyushin jets crash in mysterious circumstances after taking off from Domodedovo Airport. One, carrying holiday makers to Sochi, where Putin also was vacationing, is destroyed within minutes of the other. There are immediate suggestions of terrorism, especially as the Chechen presidential elections are imminent. The suspicion that air defense forces might have brought down the planes is instantly dismissed as "unlikely" by an official, who adds, "This is rather a scenario for American blockbuster films." And now, possibly, a Russian one too.

I have an eerie, uncomfortable feeling thinking back on that day of filming at Domodedovo, having seen the planes and passengers innocently going about their daily business. Security has been severely tightened, our shoot probably being the last to be given such free access. Two Chechen women suicide bombers are eventually suspected of the crime, while six lucky passengers, removed from one of the flights for being drunk, are living proof of another Russian saying that "God takes care of the intoxicated."

In the United States, film industry newspapers report that the director of *Night Watch*, Timur Bekmambetov, has been signed to make an English-language sequel to his monstrously successful movie in a deal with Twentieth Century Fox, which naturally hopes that they have staked the Next Big Thing. How will he fare in the vampire world of Hollywood? The recent track record for émigré Russian directors is rather bloodless. Andrei Konchalovsky made a mark, but not as emphatic as that in his native land, while the distinguished Elem Klimov was unable to get studio support for his proposed film of Bulgakov's *The Master and Margarita*. Will Bekmambetov's outrageous creativity be similarly sapped by bottom-lining studio "suits," or will his relationship with the Hollywood facility that crafted many of *Night Watch*'s very special effects cross-fertilize into a wider domain? What seems certain, however, is that the Russians—and their box office potential—are coming.

Back in the real world, in perhaps one of the most shocking terrorist attacks of all in the town of Beslan in the contentious Ossetia region of southern Russia, Chechen separatists slaughter several hundred women and children after taking more than a thousand hostage on September 1, that sacred first day of school. Special forces units, similar to those we had filmed with, are employed in the situation's bloody resolution.

Putin faces a major crisis as, for the first time, his cast-iron reputation for being the agent of stability begins to crack. Before the Beslan atrocity, polls revealed an overwhelming desire for the Chechen issue to be resolved by peaceful means. Now, how will he react? "This is an attack against all of us," the president tells a shocked nation that resembles a post-9/11 America. "We ride on the subway and think it is for the last time," a Moscow priest confides. "We gather in a church and think it is our last liturgy." How strange that Russia and America should again be held in a mutual balance of destruction—this time by the insidious, invisible forces of international terrorism. Will the town of Beslan be the only one forced to enlarge its cemetery?

A year ago Red Square was closed to us because of the terrorist threat; now, ironically for the very same reason, the huge symbolic place is allowed to fill up with thousands of citizens protesting this threat to their society. Putin responds—on the anniversary of 9/11, no less—by tightening his grip on the country, justifying his elimination of checks and balances by citing the need for a stronger central authority. How long before the refrain "Back in the USSR" becomes the leitmotiv of the times?

There are fears for the continued success of the confidence-driven stock market. Putin seems to like commerce but not businessmen. He approves of the law but not independent legal practitioners. He tolerates the media, but only journalists who endorse his policies. In a sense, he himself is a paradigm of the problems facing Russia, serving as he does as an efficient bridge between the Soviet past and the capitalist future. But some of the bridge's foundations are weak, and one key support has been mined with explosives by nationalist rebels in retaliation for his ruthless suppression of their dissent. Its toll keepers demand bribes and let only the chosen cross over. Will Putin's Napoleonic ambitions meet their Borodino, or will there one day be a giant statue to him too on the Moscow River?

September 2004 marks my fortieth anniversary as a professional actor, and I celebrate by heading back with Pat to Europe and another job—this time a good role in a film called *Icon*, to be made in Bulgaria. Based on Frederick Forsyth's thriller about political maneuvering in a vaguely contemporary Russia, it comes replete with the theft of a potentially devastating bioagent—the equivalent of the stolen nuclear suitcase that gives such a frisson of plausible thrills to *Moscow Heat*. Rather like a straight-faced version of my *Austin Powers* character, I'm again the smooth British intelligence chief, while Patrick Swayze plays a heroic American agent out to save the world. Needless to say, matters have reverted to form, and the chief villain is a Russian.

Sofia, basking in a golden autumn sun, reveals itself to be a charming city, poised between shabby and smart—between its recent impoverished past and its potentially prosperous future. Gypsy encampments can still be seen alongside modern high-rises. No doubt Bulgaria will be transformed as swiftly as other former Soviet satellites. The Cyrillic script, purportedly invented here, is already being challenged by an invasion of Latin alphabet signage, giving the place an agreeably schizoid feel.

The city makes a good substitute for Moscow, where *Icon* is mostly set. Indeed, the Russian church glimpsed outside the window of the military club where we film sustains the illusion, as does the nearby Alexander Nevsky Cathedral—a gift from Russia—with its traditional cupolas and domes. The company has clinched it all by filming for a week in Moscow, even managing to use Red Square with, incredibly, a tank and a mob of protestors on it.

Another gift from the mother country is Sofia's town hall, now seeming sadly truncated without its steeple-topping red star. A sweet story was recounted in Communist times about a man leaning his bicycle against a wall of this building. Told by an official to remove it because a Soviet delegation was about to arrive, he replies, "Don't worry—I'll lock it up!" Just by the cathedral there's a flea market, with Soviet memorabilia vying for sale with Nazi trophies. Sofia is a compact, manageable city built on several layers of civilization and provides a Sunday of enjoyable sightseeing.

We resume filming beside a lovely lake in continued good weather. As in Russia, the exhausted crew takes advantage of the late autumn sunshine. Here, too, young girls seem to be an indispensable part of the unit, but this time my driver speaks good English and fills me in on details of life here. Driving home, he points out a car pulled over for speeding, whose driver now faces the choice of paying an instant fine or having his license taken away. No choice, in fact.

An important factor for normalizing society to meet a new European standard is the elimination—or marginalization, like the Mafia in America—of corruption. As in Russia, where it is reputed to cost business billions of dollars a year, it is still endemic. I was encouraged, though, to hear an interview with Valery Gergiev, the great conductor of the Kirov. A few decades ago, he claims, the balance between the dark and the light, between the forces of corruption and enlightenment, was ninety to ten. It is now more even—but with a long way to go.

At least the many studios around Sofia are booming, as film productions that a few years ago might have gone to the Czech Republic or Hungary have moved farther east in search of cheaper costs. Where next—Kazakhstan? Perhaps Afghanistan? Hollywood's "runaway production" will perhaps soon be checked at the source by the signing in October of US legislation giving extensive tax breaks for modestly budgeted films and even better deals for those made at home in "distressed" areas of the country. So, in the future, one might be seeing more of the rural American south than urban eastern Europe.

Back home, I meet with Alexander in our usual Westwood restaurant, where he enjoys his invariable lunch, so improbable for a bodybuilder, of caesar—or should it now be czar—salad with double chicken, no cheese or croutons. This time his gift is a Putin matryoshka doll. I'm delighted, as I coveted one when in Russia. It opens to reveal in succession almost all the politicians mentioned in this narrative, with a tiny Rasputin at its heart. All are contained inside Putin's appropriately tough, inflexible wooden frame.

We talk about the impending premiere in Moscow and the possibility of my returning for it. It seems extraordinary to be making other travel plans so soon after stowing the battered suitcases, but I have now come to accept that this is part of the York karma—not to be resisted but embraced. Apparently Parliament vodka is anxious to further promote the film in which its product has such a stellar presence. Again I'm impressed by Alexander's grasp of the realities and challenges of production and his willingness to approach things in an unconventional way. That economics degree of his is being put to good use.

But first, I'm curious to see the fully finished English version (the Moscow premiere will be in dubbed Russian), so Pat and I attend a screening of *Moscow Heat* at the American Film Market in Santa Monica. This reunites us not only with Katya and Alexander but with Sasha Izotov, who has flown over for the occasion. My heart does a nervous drum roll of its own as the lights go down, but when they come up again some ninety furiously paced minutes later, I experience both relief and pleasure. The film works! The sound effects and score have added immeasurably, as has the extra looped dialogue. Above all, the film looks impressive up on the big screen. We all retire for a celebratory lunch. Sasha informs me that billboards will soon be going up, accompanied by television promotion. We raise glasses to our reunion in Moscow.

Десять · 10

Red Carpet in Red Square

Boast not on your way to Moscow, but on your return.
— RUSSIAN PROVERB

Like some doomed creature plunging from a medieval heaven to the other, nether place, our flight descends through a gilded mantle of clouds that cushions the shock of arriving down below in a world of thick gray gloom. Except this other place is no fiery hot spot but a decidedly cold one. Snow swirls along the icy runway as we—Pat, Alexander, Katya, and I—pull into Sheremetyevo Airport once again. My wish to see Moscow in the snow has been granted. In fact, the fates have been overly generous—more snow fell the previous day, November 20, than at any other time for this season during the past twenty years.

Arrival formalities completed, we are greeted by a young maiden wearing a gilt headpiece and a flimsy blue robe who offers us ceremonial bread and salt as those inevitable cameras flash anew. Sasha Izotov, with a large bouquet of flowers for Pat, is there to meet us with several members of his staff, who whisk away our baggage. But, consistent with our filming schedule, there is a technical delay—this time because the Nevskys' luggage, including Katya's carefully chosen dress for the premiere, has failed to travel with them from Los Angeles.

While Katya applies herself to the multiple form filling, Alexander escorts us to the limousine outside, which, in its stretched, moon-roofed, cocktail-bar'd opulence is even longer than any hitherto encountered here. Inside a journalist lies in wait, tape recorder at the ready. And so it begins. We talk about our film as coherently and enthusiastically as jet lag will allow. In any case, there's not much to observe of the passing scene through the fogged windows, and great banks of freshly plowed snow impede both view and progress.

This time Pat and I are staying at the Metropole Hotel, just opposite the Bolshoi Theater, and we pull up at its simple side door. The former grand entrance, with its magnificent tiled art nouveau facade, is now stranded amid swirling traffic in a no-man's-land on the busy main street. The unassuming entry plays up the magnificence of what lies within—a palace of marble and gold, with elegant furnishings, rich carpeting, and an elevator enclosed in handcrafted glass. One immediately endearing feature is that all the meeting rooms are named after Russian writers. A few of them stare at us from the walls, along with other famous patrons, as we pass by en route to our suite. It turns out to be equally grand, replete with stiff-backed carved furniture, a chandelier, and a solemnly ticking pendulum clock. The bathroom has been squeezed to accommodate a sauna, although the nearly tropical warmth of the hotel would seem to make such a luxury redundant.

While Pat settles in, I go out for the traditional walk to Red Square. Hatless and gloveless, I am totally unprepared for the shock of the numbing cold that sends me retreating past the baubled Christmas tree, like a shivering remnant of Boney's Grande Armée.

What an extraordinary people the Russians must be to prosper in such inimical conditions. If this is challenging, what on earth can Siberia be like? I remember the fur hat I bought here thirty years ago as a tourist souvenir and curse myself for not bringing it with me.

We dine in the Metropole's restaurant, a gargantuan room with a lofty glass ceiling that is just as I imagine a stateroom on the *Titanic* to be. A singer in traditional costume accompanied by a small orchestra adds to the surreal feeling of being hurled back into this half-familiar, half-alien, time-warped world.

Daylight comes with unexpected sunshine and blue skies and the revelation that the Moskva Hotel across the square has indeed been razed—just one of the many Soviet era hostelries demolished in an unsentimental orgy of upgrading. Momentarily resisting this encroaching tide of new construction, Mayor Luzhkov once considered retaining the empty space revealed on a permanent basis. The unlovely Rossiya Hotel is also due to vanish from the scene as efficiently as an out-of-favor politician used to be airbrushed out of group photographs. The view of the Kremlin that it ruined for so long will now be liberated—hopefully permanently, though there's already talk of a replacement complex.

Hotels are being torn down faster than they are being rebuilt, endangering Moscow's ambition to host the 2012 Olympic Games, since there will be a shortage of suitable accommodations. At present there are only 5,000 four- or five-star rooms, contrasted with the 126,000 of megahost Las Vegas. Preservation is the latest order of the day: one of the landmark Seven Sisters, the Hotel Ukraina, is being upgraded to international standards, its warren of 800 rooms decimated. Meanwhile the Metropole is fully booked, testifying to the fact that Moscow now enjoys one of the highest occupancy rates in the industry.

We have breakfast in the vast dining room, which swallows patrons as a whale does sprats. A cold daylight filters through the glass ceiling as we are seated by a rather chill-inducing ornamental fountain. Last night's musical group has been replaced by a lone harpist, plucking away in a pink evening gown. Food of every possible taste and texture is liberally laid out like props for a film orgy. Grim experience motivates me to take the fresh juices as well as the more substantial winter fuel.

Pat is embarked on a one-woman smiling campaign, provoking some double takes and the occasional response in kind. Natasha, our slim young interpreter, supplies a plausible reason for the grimness. Here, she explains, people are required to look as serious as possible in passport photos. When American friends saw hers, they sympathized with her for being ill that day and showed off their own beaming versions. Deciding to remedy the situation, Natasha smiled broadly for her next passport image, only to be asked by Russian friends if she had been unwell when it was taken. Worse still, passport officials were reluctant to accept it, and ever since she has been obliged to replicate the grin whenever entering the country, just to confirm her identity!

Alexander joins me for more interviews by the press and television. The hotel management has allowed us to set up a little studio in one of the huge hallways, to the amusement of passing maids. At one point we pose for outdoor photographs against the background of a sunstruck Bolshoi Theater. Shostakovich's *Lady Macbeth of Mtsensk,* which so compromised his creativity by inflaming Stalin's ire, is playing this evening. Having recently interpreted the composer, I would love to attend a performance, but there is no time. All this interviewing is hard work, especially keeping the conversations fresh and unrepetitive, and at the end of the day we have to attend a party at a local restaurant hosted by Parliament vodka.

On the way there we pass huge posters for the film, known here as *Moskovskaya Zhara,* and even video screen presentations. Outside our destination a hardy crowd has assembled around a huge ice fountain shaped like a Parliament bottle—the *ne plus ultra* of product placement—from which libations liberally flow. I'm reminded of the one ordered by a certain U.S. executive who attracted recent news headlines for throwing a party that included an ice statue of Michelangelo's David pissing vodka. For some reason, soldiers dressed in old-fashioned greatcoats and helmets fire muskets into the air as toasts and speeches are made. I contribute one about the reliability and transparent performance of our spirited, liquid co-star who, despite hogging the camera, never answered back when taking direction. It is so cold that a Parliamentary infusion becomes indispensable to keep faculties of brain and speech connected.

The last time I saw so many bottles of vodka or tasted their contents was when a friend, Dr. Robert Gale, returned to LA from treating the victims of the Chernobyl disaster. Mostly homemade (Russians even have a horseradish vodka), they came in every color and proof, and the hangover they induced was of positively nuclear intensity.

Inside we mingle with an eclectic mix of politicians, entertainers, and party personalities against a backdrop of karaoke singing, ferociously loud music, and flashing cameras. Again we try to avoid being caught eating, even posting the bodyguard to block this unphotogenic activity. Eventually the sleek limo, as silent as a sleigh, returns us to our hotel haven. Here the loudest sound is the ticking of the clock, reminding us not to retire as a freshly wakened California awaits our calls.

The next day, Tuesday, is blessed with continued sun and Pat and I venture out over the icy pavements to Red Square, passing people equally fortified against the still bitter cold. Fur coats are worn unapologetically, some with great, enviable hoods. I hear that Lenin's tomb is about to close while its moth-eaten occupant, immune alike to frost and fashion, gets a change of clothes. Now more a curiosity than a cult, maybe one day he'll defy the tourist trade and return to what was once Leningrad, as was supposedly his dying wish. The summer queues and crowds have gone, liberating each remarkable vista, and the city wears a wintry beauty.

Temporarily free of interviews, we request a car to take us on a brief tour of this manifest boomtown. There's more new construction to provide rich material for the lavish Russian edition of *Architectural Digest.* As the statistician predicted, traffic seems to have doubled since our last visit, with Russia's answer to the Hummer, the armored $144,000 Kombat, adding to the crush. Everything seizes up completely when a staid old tram sideswipes yet another car. It's sad to see the shell of the burned-out Manezh, although there is encouraging talk of it being restored. One challenging aspect of the rebuilding is that modern technology seems incapable of duplicating the original ceiling.

At another blaze an exasperated firefighter is reported to have complained, "Do you really expect there to be hydrants and extinguishers? This is Russia—people don't give a damn." His negativity is echoed by Natasha when I ask her if young people are optimistic about the future. Nothing will change, she says, because people basically don't want change. As long as they have their beer and TV, they'll support whoever is in power. We also discuss the alarming new statistic that the small group of rich people at the top of the wealth pyramid now owns fifteen times more than the huge group of poor at the bottom.

Yet the demand for sushi has driven the price of a California roll to $17. We stick to an old favorite, stopping off at the Café Pushkin for its warming borscht. I then return with Alexander to Ostankino for a television show. Security seems tighter, my driver's license being scrutinized before I'm allowed in. Alexander, still in his travel clothes, has been told there's only "a faint chance" that his bags will arrive tomorrow. I would offer him some blinkers, if only I knew what they are!

After the show, we are trapped in another traffic jam of home-going vehicles, this one exacerbated by the policeman who arbitrarily switches the traffic light to red to allow a Kremlin bigwig a speedy exit from Savior Gate. Although I'm assured that the same red light routine is also practiced in Washington, there seems to be little difference here from the time when official Zil limousines used to race imperiously down the center lanes. Putin is even more triumphalist, traveling in his black Mercedes 600 Pullman in a heavily armed cortege, with roads closed and cleared in front of him, to and from his estate in the exclusive Rublyovka district. Here Yeltsin, Gorbachev, and—surprising for this frequent critic of Western materialism—Solzhenitsyn also have homes.

At least the enforced halt gives us a chance to talk and listen to the radio spots advertising our film. Alexander tells me that he's been looking for a Gollywood-style red carpet for the premiere, something unusual here even though there is now a thriving domestic industry with 120 feature films being shot in 2004 alone. Mosfilm has just announced that it plans to build one of the largest film studio complexes in Europe. Two imported films will be opening tomorrow in competition with ours: *Bridget Jones's Diary* and Oliver Stone's *Alexander*. The first is somewhat discounted as a "woman's picture" but, in the duel of action heroes, will our Alexander be proved equally great? The *Moscow Heat* DVD will be released remarkably soon—in mid-December—to prevent pirates from peddling a stolen version first. Robert Madrid will be coming over to help with its promotion, following a short visit by Richard Tyson to similarly boost our efforts.

That evening, I take Pat to the Vogue Café and look in vain for my former dinner partners. Even the Carpetbagger is absent, and

I resist the temptation to check to see if he ever settled our bill. It is enjoyable to be among so many lively people, even though it's shocking to realize that the cost of our meal is equal to a month's wages elsewhere in Russia. A new no-smoking rule is in effect but, as in most of Europe, it seems to be honored more in the breach than the observance. Perhaps this helps explain why this year's death rate is predicted to outpace the birth rate by at least 50 percent, ensuring a life expectancy equal to that of Bangladesh.

Wednesday morning is devoted to a pair of contrasting interviews—one for the new Russian version of the popular *Hello* magazine, the other for the more serious *Izvestia* newspaper. The latter is still a beautifully laid-out broadsheet, putting the famous London *Times,* now shrunk to humble tabloid format, to shame. The rather dour young lady from *Izvestia,* a prime candidate for Pat's smiling campaign, asks many politically oriented questions, and I'm happy to report from the recent battleground of the American election. Both interviews are a curious amalgam of the guarded and the open, the edited and the uninhibited. I try to be as engaging as this process of unburdening to complete strangers allows. It is arm's length intimacy, and yet this is how Paul McCartney, Gregory Peck—and, not least, myself—met their spouses.

Flagging toward the end of the morning, I think enviously of David Hemmings's interview technique. Like that inventive Kremlin guide, David would spice up his responses with all manner of tall-storied inventions. The only constant distraction comes from the photographers. The digital era's exchange of expensive film for unlimited pixels has unleashed a feeding frenzy of flashing.

Pat and I are requested to be ready and dressed in our premiere clothes for an inordinately early pickup at 3:15 P.M. This is because a 4:00 P.M. press conference has been scheduled prior to the start of the film at 7:30. But at the appointed hour nothing happens, and we wait in puzzled ignorance. Our room becomes an ornate cell. I should be inured to this by now. What has happened to my Zen acceptance of all things untoward? "I wasted time, and now doth time waste me": Shakespeare's anguished verse springs cruelly to mind as I catalog all the things we could be doing with this precious time—visiting the old Lenin Museum, for example, which now houses the National Center for Contemporary Art, retrieving e-mail, or even taking a sauna.

People live on cell phones here—why can't someone at least use one now? Why is truth so imprecise, and time of such elastic value? Some of the psychosomatic symptoms that afflicted me during filming, such as the nagging back and guts, show signs of returning. Pat confesses belated sympathy for my more frustrated phone calls home last summer.

Eventually, in the midst of the evening rush hour, transportation arrives and we crawl to the press conference, where a roomful of journalists has obviously been kept waiting too. I'm genuinely apologetic, but no one seems unduly put out. Surely they don't consider this tardiness to be typical Gollywood behavior? After what is less a conference and more a compressed chat, we all board the limo and head for the theater. Alexander and Katya are dressed in finery liberated just in time from their errant bags. At the cavernous Pushkinsky there is indeed a red carpet laid before us, now scuffed and soiled by countless slush-laden shoes.

Their owners await inside. I would never have risked their patience for so long but, like the press conference journalists and unlike me, the large audience seems amazingly tolerant. Perhaps we are all waiting for Putin to show up, although he's probably busy with his plans to merge the imprisoned Khodorkovsky's beleaguered Yukos oil company, once the most successful private enterprise in postcommunist Russia, into a state conglomerate. There are speeches and presentations, and a bevy of lissome young girls parades across the stage laden with white roses. I take it that this symbolic obeisance to the heraldic flower of the House of York is fully intended and not just a happy accident. The lights eventually dim and the world premiere of *Moskovskaya Zhara* begins.

The first thing that impresses is the remarkably effective Russian dubbing; I'm astonished at my own fluency. Although I rather miss his English accent, Alexander has been given a sonorous, gravelly basso by the actor who habitually revoices Schwarzenegger. Unavailable for the Russian sound mix, Alexander no doubt appreciates this added connection to his idol. There are laughs—some unintentional as when, outside Moscow University, a character remarks that the airport is close by. My scene with the grandfather gets a good response—and there is even applause in places, especially when Alexander returns my son's ring taken by the mobster. One of the more unsubtle product placements provokes loud amusement, somewhat vindicating my objections. When the lights go up again, our efforts seem to be well received and there are several generous compliments.

Afterward everyone retires, this time at an appropriate hour, to the Casus Conus nightclub. Despite being rushed up to the inner sanctum at the top of the building, we are swiftly engulfed by the waiting public. We sign autographs, shake hands, and pose for photos. One guest, an intelligent political journalist, compliments the film's pace and performances. He also confides that he used to be admired for speaking English but, in the present political climate, plays down this accomplishment, especially when traveling. No less a commentator than Mikhail Gorbachev recently confirmed this anti-Americanism, saying it had reached a scale too large for the United States to ignore; for Uncle Sam to continue to act unilaterally "would not work as logical and serious politics." How long before we Americans become the villains in Russian movies?

I find it almost impossible to eat and greet; with little nourishment since lunchtime, it's the *Moscow Heat* diet revisited, with not even a Snickers bar to stave off the pangs! I'm happy to run into Lina and Katrina again, the latter wearing another minimalist outfit that would easily pass Jeff's criteria for Maria's skimpy wardrobe. Having graduated from the Vakhtangov, Katrina is now teaching and working as a film professional, even being involved with *Icon* when it filmed here in many of the same locations we used. It will be interesting to compare results: big studio versus little independent. She also played a gangster's moll in our movie, tussling on a pool table with Alexander, "whose wrists were larger than my biceps—in four-inch stiletto heels too!"

The following morning I'm transported to a different TV studio for what I assume is yet another promotional interview. It's so cold that one of the limo doors is frozen shut. I should have taken this as an omen and declined to get in. A bright sun highlights the columns of steam rising from the city's power stations into the vodka-clear sky. Passing the Bentley distributor not far from the new Rolls-Royce agency, we drive by shining snow banks and the shimmering domes of a Kremlin now resembling an elaborate sugarplum and gingerbread Christmas decoration.

It is good to know that Malcolm Forbes's Fabergé eggs will be returning home, financed by a $90 million private initiative. I wonder if the Fabergé "stamp moistener," which so elegantly spared the royal tongue, sold recently by New York's "A La Vieille Russie," will eventually join them. London auction houses are also busy selling Russian art back to Russians, including a Repin painting repatriated for nearly $2 million. By the same token, the Iron Curtain tended to prevent most contemporary art from leaving Russia and there is now a mass exodus of such works.

As he lives nearby, Alexander and I have agreed to meet at the studio, but there's no sign of him there. During the usual tea and makeup routine, I'm astonished to discover that I will indeed be appearing on this morning's show, but not to discuss movies. My duty will be to determine if the main guests, two young ladies of contrasting sexual proclivities, are as they claim Huntress or Hunted. Since it's too late to politely back out, I reassume my Zen mask of cosmic acceptance. I wait an hour for my tardy co-star to arrive—as does a whole studio audience with the same resigned patience as our premiere patrons.

The producer decides to start without Alexander, but an apologetic phone call keeps us there until his eventual arrival, when we are bundled onto the cheerfully bright set. The show is hosted by a former actress who found her present employment on TV when the film industry collapsed. Our man hunter, appropriately dressed in dominatrix boots, and our diminutive victim take their places under the spotlights. Besides Alexander and me, their inquisitors include a rumpled, black-leathered young poet called Vadim who reads a lengthy ode, the gist of which seeming to be that a woman is best handled by dosing her with unlimited amounts of vodka and beer. Asked about my own attitude to the fair sex, I do everything in my power to answer indirectly, while Alexander manages to twist his every response into a promotion for *Moscow Heat*.

The audience then joins the debate, including one of the few other males present, a psychiatrist who sounds more like a psychopath, and the usual assembly of neat housewives like the ones who are presumably watching the show. Actors are supposed to be students of the human condition and, to a certain extent, the revelations are fascinating, although I dislike anyone claiming to be a victim as much as I do a predatory female. Also, it's so warm in the studio that I have to struggle to stay focused. It all seems fairly innocuous and, who knows, may even sell a few tickets in Tomsk and Novosibirsk.

Afterward Alexander quickly disarms me by explaining that our presence this morning was quid pro quo for the station airing many promotions for our film. We then drive from what seems to be one end of Moscow to the other, returning to Ostankino. In the turgid traffic, it's like inching up a frozen river in an icebreaker. But with a glistening sun still embracing the city, the two-hour transition provides visual joys. We pass many interesting places, including the U.S. embassy compound, a little mini-America with its own malls, fast-food outlets and, no doubt, overweight patrons.

A sort of current affairs-cum-variety program, the afternoon TV show turns out to be equally tangential to the promotional job in hand. A dozen fellow guests are lined up on couches surrounding a rectangular pit inhabited by a prowling, dapper-suited pit bull of a host barking information and questions. He is so vociferous that he drowns out the translation being fed into my buzzing earpiece, so my responses are mostly based on hopeful guesswork. An agricultural minister talks about the price of staples and I'm about to contribute that everything, apart from staples, seems to cost more here than in Los Angeles when the topic switches abruptly to stand-up comedy.

This apparently is the new Russian sensation, and from samples given, it seems to parallel our own sense of humor: "Someone asks an airline to send three suitcases to three different cities, only to be informed that this is impossible. Why, comes the response, you did that to mine last week!" Given his recent experience, however, I doubt if Alexander finds this funny. A famous comedian leads the discussion and I'm tempted to add that we may all share the same sense of humor, but we definitely lack the same timing. I'm glad I withhold this little barb, though, as he makes a gracious compliment about *Cabaret*.

It is sobering to realize that despite its superficial political content, this is one of the few TV shows left to go out live. All others

are edited, and any frank discussions of controversial issues are
suppressed. Our favorite Ekho Moskvy radio station remains the
last national independent broadcaster.

After the show I meet up with Pat at the Twin Pigs, a local restaurant beloved of the TV community whose gates are flanked by two
giant polychrome porkers. Our plan is to have an early supper and
then put in the requested appearance at the Mrs. Russia contest being held nearby. After two makeups and studio sessions I'm beginning to feel a trifle unfresh, but a return to the hotel for a shower
and change seems unfeasable in present traffic conditions. The contest is supposed to begin at 6:30 P.M., but by the time we arrive the
main event is again a press-packed party. Everyone is smartly
dressed—even the comedian from the last show is there changed
into an elegant new outfit—but when I try to minimally tidy up
and at least comb my hair I'm caught in a hail of flash photos. I can
see tomorrow's headlines: "Man Takes Off Sweater. Lives!"

All this inflames a lurking irritation that our promised brief
encounter with the show has again been misrepresented. Discovering that I am expected to be a judge for the whole nationally
televised event, despite all my carefully acquired acting skills, I
find it hard to hide displeasure. "Is Michael York pissed off?" a
perceptive guest enquires of Pat. I pull myself together and answer, to the best of my still limited experience, a question already
extensively rehearsed this morning: "What do you think of Russian women?" What I would really like to ask is why they don't
demand more equality with men. Why do they marry and di-
vorce more quickly than women in other countries in the region?

Sasha Izotov, arriving with a genuine reason to party, interrupts.
It's his birthday and he is serenaded with the local version of the familiar refrain. I only hope that our film reviews will provide him
with a "just-what-I-wanted" present. Fortunately the protracted delay in starting the contest works in our favor. After sitting in the half-

filled auditorium for some time, Pat and I seize the chance to depart before any premature exit is recorded on television. Leaving Alexander, the former Mr. World, to somehow work *Moscow Heat* into his selection of the ideal Mrs. Russia, we escape into the night and back to suitcases demanding a repack before tomorrow's departure.

Fresh snow is blanketing the ground when we peer through the heavy drapes next morning. It's early—the breakfast harpist is still tuning up. The newspapers are full of the extraordinary events surrounding the disputed election in Russia's "near-abroad," Ukraine. Putin's attempts to steer the result toward his favored pro-Russian candidate appear to have been rebuffed by a genuine grassroots democracy movement. Although such public action has never had a prime place in Russian politics, this suggests that perhaps there is an alternative to the Putin formula of toothless opposition and media coupled with crony politics. The old knee-jerk cliché that only this autocratic, managed version of democracy is acceptable to the Slav soul now seems untenable.

I wonder if the people are still behind Putin, or if he has missed his chance. It's hard to tell as public criticism goes mostly unheard on late-night talk radio. And there's much to complain about: the *Economist* magazine reports that in 2004 the quality of life actually declined in Russia, plunging the nation to a lowly 105th ranking out of 111 other countries.

Inside the *Moscow Times* a review of our film carries the promising headline, "Russia in Action." Both generous and discriminating, it shares my chief reservation about the finished result, the "intense" product placement. On the plus side, both John Aronson and Gib Jaffe are commended for their work and I'm flattered to be complimented on my "nimble" contribution to the action scenes. But there's no time to dwell on the details. The limo is at the door awaiting our return to Sheremetyevo and our Aeroflot flight back to the States.

There's no escape from cinema: the plane is full of filmmakers heading to a festival of Russian movies in New York, with even the minister of culture aboard. I notice someone reading a Russian review of our film but I'm too cowardly to ask for a translation. Bertold Brecht insisted that "every actor exists to be criticized," but often this is more maliciously wounding than usefully instructive. Working with Tennessee Williams in one of his last plays in the 1970s, I remember him referring to the critics as "the firing squad that waits in every city." But it was another playwright, the Irishman Brendan Behan, who most vividly dismissed them by comparing critics to harem eunuchs, as they could never do what they saw being done all around them!

We take off from a field as white as a cinema screen and, wheeling over the immense, mysterious land, eventually return to the sun that lures us back to the new world. There's ample time to reflect on the fate of *Moscow Heat.* Perhaps it is but the first of many such international collaborations, designed more for box office appeal than ideological allure. I suspect there will be more, especially if the sclerotic visa situation is improved. Film can be an outstanding communicator, fulfilling that Shakespearean dramatic imperative of "holding the mirror up to nature." As events in Ukraine demonstrate, it's risky to leave international relationships to politicians.

Between the Hong Kong-style action and the Gollywood-style drama, *Moscow Heat* provides a little of what Peter the Great—that celebrated reformist of Muscovite pretensions—sought when he spoke of opening a Russian window onto the outside world. Except that our movie has done it in reverse, presenting a window, however small and at times obscured, through which the outside world can glimpse a unique era in the history of the beguiling, infuriating, irresistible Russian nation.

Afterword:
The Great Game

I n early January 2005, like the proverbial bad penny, the wily Carpetbagger turns up at a Los Angeles party. Obviously burned by his own Moscow heat, he regales me with plans for U.S. film productions, while I reassume my Easter Island statue demeanor. After the ritual Golden Globe Awards, attended by both Alexander and his hero and role model, Governor Arnold Schwarzenegger, Alexander and I meet for another ritual lunch—same venue, same menu—on LA's west side. He has quite a story to tell. It helps explain and even excuse the episodes that so puzzled and provoked Pat and me during our recent Moscow visit.

Apparently when Alexander arrived for the premiere, he lost not only baggage but almost his control of his film's promotion. Because of yet another in a long line of misunderstandings, the *Moscow Heat* posters were not put up until the previous day, so advance publicity was minimal. To save the situation, he went into overdrive, taking meetings and arranging interviews around the fast-ticking clock—hence his mystifying absences and preoccupations. The first weekend's business reflected the negligibility of the advertising, but then, as word of mouth spread and our press interviews gradually appeared, the situation began to reverse.

Normally a film's ticket sales diminish in the subsequent weeks of its run, but for *Moscow Heat* the opposite proved true. It actually gained business incrementally over the month it was shown theatrically, contributing to the end-of-year estimate of an almost 60 percent rise in Russian box office takings. Reflecting their newfound popularity, Moscow's movie theaters stay open all day—and some all night.

As a result of his heroic efforts, Alexander was able to make a lucrative sale to the leading state television channel. Proof of the film's success, meanwhile, was egregiously evident from the many pirated versions rushed into circulation. One was a piece of shameless handheld thievery, snatched at the premiere, that included all the preliminary ceremonies and speeches. Another was stolen from a subsequent showing, and there was a more stable tripod version. Yet another was pilfered from the official DVD. When this last appeared, it sold out in two days, and more had to be quickly issued. Serious legal measures are finally being enforced to combat piracy, with substantial fines and prison sentences being handed out.

Alexander's problems, however, were not over. In order to make the imminent TV showing possible, he had to supply a special digital tape. Normally it takes a week for this to be made, which would have meant missing the TV deadline, but he managed to persuade the postproduction supervisor to supply it in two days—a minor miracle, considering that everything had shut down for the Christmas holiday.

The film was shown on Channel 1, the leading television station that was also responsible for *Night Watch,* on January 3, 2005. After being heavily promoted, it attracted a huge audience and good reviews. The Parliament vodka people were delighted. Despite the ban on TV advertising of alcohol, the film was shown uncut—product placements and all! With such encouraging box office numbers and notices, Alexander now had the means to pursue his long-term strategy and make a good deal with a U.S. distributor. An advertisement duly appears in *Variety*, drawing attention to the film's box office success.

The growing importance of DVD and video sales reflects a remarkable change in the income of the film industry. In the United States in the mid-1980s, box office constituted 70 percent of revenues, with electronic versions adding the remaining income. Today the situation and the statistics are reversed: DVDs and home videos now earn the lion's share of the market, with theatrical sales making up the total. Now only 10 percent of Americans—mostly teenagers—go out to the movies, with the rest preferring to be entertained at home. The main broadcast networks, moreover, are owned by a handful of corporations that also run the film studios. With their insatiable amusement maw requiring constant filling, the balance has now been tipped toward the production of electronic media.

Back in the equally entertaining world of politics, Victor Yushchenko becomes president of Ukraine. Among his first official acts is a trip to the Kremlin to reconcile with President Putin. In trying to block the poisoned, pockmarked hero's democratic election, Putin was dealt a serious political reversal. When I ask a Russian friend why his country was still employing such Cold War capers as poisoning opponents, he remonstrates, "You kidding me? If it had been done by Russian, guy would be dead!" Meanwhile Freedom House, the respected human rights watchdog

organization, reclassifies Russia as "not free." A taxi driver originally from Minsk, who picks me up on a Dallas trip, confirms the
growing inability to make economic or political choices: "Over
there you can buy everything, but you can afford nothing."

At the end of the month, Presidents Bush and Putin meet in
Bratislava, performing agilely in a TV debate about their respective interpretations of that abused, misunderstood concept, democracy. Bush's awe-shucks affability wrapped up in a quaint
religiosity—so reminiscent of the holy fool beloved of Russian
literature—contrasts strongly with the icy self-control of his professed soulmate. Is this another "road to airport" misunderstanding or something much more significant and divisive? Or is it yet
another round in the geopolitical Great Game, one dictated by
the significance of Ukraine as a conduit for the oil and gas now
gushing from the Caspian fields?

In early March an interesting article appears in *Variety* about a
new Russian film, *Countdown,* in which their special forces are
portrayed as heroically successful, government officials are out-
standingly efficient, and terrorist situations are resolved with minimal fuss and casualties. There is even an evil expatriate media
oligarch. All this prompts speculation that the film has Kremlin
backing, rather like the managed and packaged "news" broadcasts
that are garnering criticism for the White House. "Observers are
asking," the article continues, "whether similar aid went to last
year's *Moscow Heat.*"

I'm still trying to find out the answer to this intriguing question. What I do learn from Alexander at our next lunch meeting
is that Universal Home Video, a major player, will be releasing
our film in the United States in November. He also tells me that
on this, the twentieth anniversary of the start of perestroika,
Mikhail Gorbachev has seen *Moscow Heat* and professed to like it
too. Alexander outlines a scheme for a plausible sequel, some-

thing that most film distribution companies, perforce now geared to marketing, readily embrace because it involves selling a known commodity.

Forbes magazine publishes its latest roll call of the wealthy, revealing that the number of Russian billionaires has overtaken Japan's, climbing to twenty-seven. The thirty-six richest citizens own $110 billion, or almost a quarter of the nation's gross domestic product. Clinging to the list, despite the confiscation of his Yukos empire, is the imprisoned Mikhail Khodorkovsky, whose show trial has just ended in a predictable verdict of guilty. Mayor Luzhkov's wife, Elena, is the first Russian woman ranked among the billionaires. These include the soccer czar, Roman Abramovich, who also lives in London in a $10 million flat. With the demotion of Khodorkovsky, he is now Russia's richest man. While gold reserves stand at record levels and oil prices show an 85 percent increase over last year, the rest of the population faces the prospect of being reduced to a third world type of poverty. With the average monthly wage a measly $240, Russia is ranked just below Brazil in terms of per capita income by the World Bank.

Garry Kasparov, the world's greatest chess player, resigns, vowing to devote himself to politics and to checkmate Putin's "dictatorship." In Central Asia, the longtime strongman of Kyrgyzstan, hitherto a pawn on Russia's great board, is chased from office in a popular revolt similar to recent ones in Ukraine and Georgia. Rumblings are felt in Belarus; is it conceivable that the same shockwaves could one day set the Kremlin trembling? "Everyone understands that the big lion is dead and should not be feared," comments one political analyst. Has the cunning old beast expired, or is it merely sleeping to gather strength for more impressive exploits? Looking for an answer to this question, I accept an invitation, as unusual as it was unexpected, to attend the Eighth Russian Economic Forum to be held April 10–12 in London.

The conference begins with a dinner at the Royal Academy given by the Gmurzynska Gallery, who also happen to represent Pat as a photographer. They have lined the room with works by Chagall, Larionov, Exter, Kandinsky, Malevich, and other masters of the Russian avant-garde. We fill our eyes with beauty and our minds with conversation, fortunate to be seated with Mikhail Kasyanov, the prime minister of Russia until February 2004. With his charisma and eloquence, it is easy to see why he is being tipped as a possible next president of Russia. In addition—speaking equally impeccable English—there is Boris Fyodorov, the former deputy prime minister who, chatting about movies, tells me about seeing *Logan's Run* in a Moscow stadium. A major liberal and pro-Western player, he was responsible for supervising many of the reforms that transformed Russia from a communist society.

We discuss such issues as the influence of Russia's emerging middle class, the establishment of firm regulations free of red tape, and the need for people to take more responsibility—the old initiative problem mentioned earlier. A recurring theme is that Russia has so much more to offer than oil and weapons and that things are never as bad as they seem. Inquiring about the ongoing gagging of the Russian media, for example, I'm asked how truly free I consider the U.S. press to be and have to admit reservations about the drift toward control by a few influential American oligarchs.

The forum is held at the Queen Elizabeth II Conference Centre in Westminster, and a sunny Monday morning finds it filled with "suits," both male and, I'm glad to see, female. One of the first to address the packed assembly is, ironically, "Red Ken" Livingstone, Yuri Luzhkov's ascetic counterpart as mayor of London. Both of us were born during the 1940s, and he touches on the solidarity with Russia that helped ensure victory in the last world war almost exactly sixty years ago.

Speaking about the need for banking reform is my friend from the Vogue Café, Petr Aven, fully justifying his recent designation as Russia's most admired financial executive. We also meet up with Viktoria Leconte, who has come over especially from Paris, and I'm delighted to be able to thank her personally for her contributions to this narrative.

In the afternoon I'm asked to join a panel to speak about the experience of filming a co-production in Russia. Among my fellow pundits are Nadia Solovieva, who runs the company that brought Paul McCartney to entertain in Red Square, and the dancer Andris Liepa, who in a cross-cultural exchange similar to my own, once guest-starred with the New York City Ballet. We talk about the need for arts sponsorship and the most appropriate sources of funding in these changing times.

It soon becomes evident that tax laws, similar to those in the United Kingdom and United States, have to be introduced in Russia in order to encourage donation from the private sector. According to another panel member, Olga Alexeeva, director of the Charities Aid Foundation in Moscow, there is not merely a popular resentment toward wealth but even a certain fearfulness in revealing the nature of individual giving. This is in stark contrast to the unrestrained flaunting of assets in America. We are a world away from Donald Trump country. Speaking feelingly of my time in Moscow, I emphasize the joys of collaboration and the potential lure of Russia to moviemakers with its competitive labor costs, playing down the differences in working methods. I touch on movie sponsorship and, bearing in mind our vodka saga, both its potential benefits and pitfalls.

What becomes quite clear from further exchanges and the up-to-the-minute literature available—including a mouth-watering booklet of the latest luxury Moscow restaurants—is that life there has already evolved in some significant respects since our film was made and even after its premiere. It's somewhat analogous to the fast-changing U.S. movie business, where observations become redundant almost as soon as they are made. Some old things, however, are new again: I'm assured that the rebuilt Manezh exhibition hall will reopen next week, albeit conspicuously minus its challenging ceiling and plus that now indispensable addition, a parking lot.

That evening guests are treated to a "Russian Rhapsody" in a Royal Albert Hall transformed into a giant cabaret with a host of tables oriented around a stage. Part of the vast space is decorated with a colorful backcloth from *Le Coq d'Or* designed by Natalia Goncharova, especially pleasing to Pat and me as we own a small costume design for the same ballet. In glamorous evening dress, the elite among Russia's decision makers and opinion formers mingle and table-hop. There's symphonic music and opera, but the main entertainment—for me at least—is provided by the many revealing encounters and conversations that are enjoyed.

There is a powerful sense that things are on the move and that a whole new era of history is even now being forged. I can almost hear the stirring strains of "Land of Hope and Glory," an anthem so frequently played in this old hall, echoing around and perhaps providing a keynote to this very special moment for the new Russia.

Acknowledgments

L ike many an effusive award-winner observed over the years, I too have a long list of thanks for a great number of people. Not least I am grateful to Frank Pearl for introducing me to the Perseus Books Group. Then there are all those who kindly read this text in its infancy and adolescence and made helpful suggestions as to its further bringing up. I am beholden to Viktoria Leconte, Katrina Faessel, and Nataliya Popovichenko for their reminiscences and insights and to Alexander Nevsky and Robert Madrid for their comments. My editor, John Radziewicz, has been a font of encouragement and perceptiveness, every opinion and suggestion expressed with an enviable wit and pertinence. I also want to thank Erin Sprague, the book's senior project editor; Trish Wilkinson, its text designer; and Alex Camlin, its cover designer. Finally, before my time runs out, I must express my indebtedness to my wife, Pat, whose critical good sense is matched only by her loving sensibility.

Index

Bulgaria, 135–137
catering and, 73
conveyance and, 76–77
India, 52, 78
Spain, 79
U.S. legislation and, 137
Yugoslavia, 7
Zagreb, 76
Location filming, *Moscow Heat*
Casus Conus nightclub, 67–68
Domodedovo Airport, 114
Kiev railway station, 89–90
Kutuzov Street, 103
Metro, 65, 109
Moscow River, 106–107, 116
police station, 95
Sparrow Hills, 107
Tsaritsino Palace, 34, 74–76,
87, 92–93, 101
Logan's Run (film), 51, 70, 160
Lollabrigida, Gina, 32
Lord of the Rings, The (film), 133
Losey, Joseph, 72, 93
Luzhkov, Yuri, 94, 97, 124, 127,
141, 159, 160

Madonna, 118
Madrid, Robert, 33, 106, 125,
131, 145
as Rudy, 4, 12, 52, 68, 74, 122
Marx Brothers, 24
Master and the Margarita, The
(Bulgakov), 62, 134
Maugham, Somerset, 32
May (mother of Michael York),
77, 79, 123

Mayor's Cup (equine event),
97–98
McCartney, Paul, 17, 146, 161
Melnick, Viktoria, 36–37
Menchikov, Oleg, 29
Meridien (hotel chain), 16
Metropole Hotel, 140–141
Mikhalkov, Nikita, 27, 29, 130
Mila (friend of York), 74
Millennium Sound Studios, 125
Milton, John, 64
Mind Benders, The (film), 72
Mortimer, Penelope, 91
Moscow
the Arbat, 86
Casus Conus nightclub, 67,
71, 148
Cathedral of Christ the
Savior, 20
City Day, 94
the Garden Ring, 62
hotel shortage, 141
House of Photography, 21, 32
Kitai Gorod, 62
Kutuzov Street, 103
Manezh building, 20, 131, 144
Novodevichy Convent and
Cemetery, 65–67
Patriarch's Ponds, 62
Pushkinsky theatre, 131
rebuilding and, 35,
131–132, 144
restaurants, 21, 27, 33, 55, 69,
144, 145, 152
Rublyovka district, 145
Seven Sisters, 91